LITTLE BAGHDAD

A MEMOIR ABOUT AN ENDANGERED PEOPLE IN AN AMERICAN CITY

WEAM NAMOU

HERMiZ
PUBLiSHING

Library of Congress Cataloging-in-Publication Data
2022922756

Namou, Weam
ISBN 978-1-945371-01-1 (paperback)
ISBN 978-1-945371-02-8 (eBook)

Little Baghdad
A Memoir About an Endangered People in an American City
(memoir)

First Edition

Published in the United States of America by:
Hermiz Publishing, Inc.
Sterling Heights, MI

10 9 8 7 6 5 4 3 2 1

Weam Namou

LITTLE BAGHDAD

A Memoir About an Endangered People in an American City

A Hermiz Publishing Book

CONTENTS

BOOKS BY WEAM NAMOU

The Feminine Art

The Mismatched Braid

The Flavor of Cultures

I Am a Mute Iraqi with a Voice

The Great American Family: A Story of Political Disenchantment

Iraqi Americans: The War Generation

Iraqi Americans: Witnessing a Genocide

Iraqi Americans: The Lives of the Artists

Healing Wisdom for a Wounded World

Mesopotamian Goddesses: Unveiling Your Feminine Power

Pomegranate

Healing Wisdom for a Wounded World
My Life-Changing Journey Through a Shamanic School
(Book 1)

Healing Wisdom for a Wounded World
My Life-Changing Journey Through a Shamanic School
(Book 2)

Healing Wisdom for a Wounded World
My Life-Changing Journey Through a Shamanic School
(Book 3)

Healing Wisdom for a Wounded World
My Life-Changing Journey Through a Shamanic School
(Book 4)

For Sudaid, Shems, Saleem, and Teddy

Acknowledgements

My gratitude to all the pioneers who have paved the way for the newer generation, and to the new generation who is continuing the responsibilities that their ancestors entrusted them with. For this particular case, it is my niece Sandy Naimou who edited this book with great love, patience, wisdom, and professionalism.

Introduction

People say we're on the verge of facing extinction. Most assume we are already extinct or melted into other groups like butter. Christians read about us in the Bible and passionately preach about us behind podiums in churches, but they do not recognize us when we stand face-to-face. To them, we look and feel intriguing and fantastical, tucked far away in ancient books. By "we" I mean the Chaldeans, a people that have over five thousand years of fascinating history. In ancient times Chaldea was part of Mesopotamia, known as "the cradle of civilization" and currently modern-day southern Iraq, where writing, the wheel, and the first cities developed around 3500 BC. It is the setting for much of the Old Testament, including the Garden of Eden, the birth of Adam and Eve, and Prophet Abraham. Several creation stories originated from that land, including the theory that the gods who descended from the heavens to Earth were actually alien visitors whose superior technology surpassed anything seen before or since then.

Today, Michigan has the largest population of Chaldeans in the world, and my hometown of Sterling Heights nicknamed "Little Baghdad," has the largest population of Chaldeans in Michigan. Chaldeans emigrated from Mesopotamia to the U.S. at the turn of the twentieth century, before the British changed its name in 1921 from Mesopotamia to Iraq after defeating the Ottoman Empire and consequently occupied the land. The majority of early Chaldean immigrants settled in Michigan where there were already Arabic speaking communities, the Lebanese and Syrian. They came in search of better social and economic opportunities, while later immigrants, especially those today, are coming to escape religious persecution.

The Chaldeans were converted to Christianity from its beginning, in the first century AD, by St. Thomas the Apostle during his passage to India. They are Catholics who still speak the Aramaic language used in Christ's time, and not only during religious ceremonies. The older generation and recently arrived refugees to the U.S. still use the language on a daily basis, though it is estimated to die within a generation.

In these five thousand years, as kingdoms rose and fell, empires expanded and contracted, and outsiders conquered and were repelled, the Chaldean people and their counterparts who have historically made tremendous contributions to human civilization, have greatly diminished in Iraq. Continuous wars and genocide over the centuries have taken their toll. The most recent genocidal atrocities have occurred as recently as 2014, when the Islamic State of Iraq and Syria (ISIS) forces spread across northern Iraq, targeting various ethnic and religious groups including the Yazidis, Shia Muslims, Assyrians, and Chaldeans, expanded the Chaldean diaspora even further.

I grew up dismissing the value of what my ancestry had to offer me, which was overshadowed by a patriarchal system that defines women from that point of view. I belonged to a younger and more modern generation, and we seemed to believe that we had life figured out. As a result, we tended to ignore the older generation's way of thinking. But shortly after I became a mother, things changed. I began searching into my personal genealogy and quickly became captivated by what I discovered about my ancestors' cultural identity, my "tribe" whose tribal ways date back thousands of years. Within a decade, I awoke to answers I'd been looking for: *Who am I? Who are my people?* I already knew where I came from—Iraq, but the physical distance between that place and myself and the human misery associated with it, kept me from truly understanding and appreciating its ancient history, culture, and language.

My research shed light on my people, and it shifted my views. In television and movies, tribal lifestyles are stereotyped as backwards or romanticized as mysterious and belonging to uncontacted tribes. I soon realized that I needed to counter these inaccurate images and that, if not documented, the rewarding side of this ancient tradition would be wasted. So in 2007, I began filming a documentary that included interviews and archival footage. I interviewed my mother, sisters, nieces, cousins, and extended relatives about how it feels, as women, to live tribally in a democracy. They shared their perspectives on how, despite their assimilation to the westerner lifestyle, they continue to be connected to instinctual tribal ways that most people repress in civilized life. They embodied an East-West wisdom that we are all in need of today. I called the documentary *Living Tribal in a Democracy.*

Over a decade has passed since I began the documentary. Between raising my two children, working on various creative projects, and caring for my elderly mother who lived with us, I worked on it sporadically. The older I got, the more I realized that it's true: We are at risk of being close to extinction. The community's cultural identity is endangered, creating urgency for me as a storyteller to shed light on its existence. *Little Baghdad* is one such effort, where I document the memories of the Chaldean people through an American city that has provided a haven for our people to survive, and more importantly, to thrive.

After my mother passed away in February 2019, I pulled the documentary off the shelves of countless projects to screen and discuss a ten-minute segment of it at Wayne State University at an event called Creative Many. The story received positive feedback and the organizers encouraged me to continue with the project. That's when I realized it was time to revisit and complete the work and write a book that, similar to the documentary, explores the role that ancient Mesopotamia played in the birth of our contemporary culture. A book that raises the following questions, which I myself as someone living tribal in a democracy, struggled with for decades and went to great lengths to find the answers: Are tribal societies models for future societies? How can tribalism and democracy coexist? Would it do the world good to return to some of the old ways, with smaller communities, a higher regard for feminine sacredness, the family system, and the elderly? How can we learn from the ancients, who are often romanticized as warriors or noble savages that we assume live in faraway or remote lands, in the jungles of Peru or in restricted areas such as Indian reservations, and neglect to see their presence in our backyard? Are we aware they do live with us here today? What was the role of women in ancient Mesopotamia, where once upon a time, kings attributed their right to rule through their official marriage to the goddess?

The material I gathered involved so much content that I decided to break it up into different books. Some of the material became the topic of my book *Mesopotamian Goddesses*, published in January 2019, a month before my mother passed away. The rest I bundled up in *Little Baghdad: A Memoir About an Endangered People in an American City*. *Little Baghdad* is a series of autobiographical essays, mostly focused on the years 2013 to 2022, when as a journalist, author, filmmaker, and a Chaldean-Iraqi immigrant, I was, unbeknownst to me, on the path to discovering my true calling.

I've since felt the strong desire to write books that share the rich, unique, mysterious, and important history and cultural heritage that's nearly forgotten, and oftentimes assumed dead. To pick up what my ancestors put down and continue, in a modern way, the narrative of the descendants of this ancient group who had influenced the entire world and are influencing American society today. We are unseen and not understood and yet we have much wisdom to offer. We have, intentionally or unintentionally, been muted even as we prosper according to the American dream in a Chaldean way. We have risen in the land that has given us sanctuary. Out of love and gratitude, in honor of our resilience, and to bring to memory the knowledge and importance of ancient ways which revered nature, feminine sacredness, and community, I want to tell our stories, which I think you will enjoy reading.

PART I

THE PAST

CHAPTER 1
MY UNEXPECTED FRENCH GUESTS

The phone rang. A welcomed interruption, since that sunny April afternoon, I had no real clarity of thought, nor the energy or inspiration necessary for the task of writing a book. The words on the computer screen hung like a laundry line. The washed laundry—not to be confused with the laundry on the computer screen—expected to be folded and happily put away. The ingredients for our dinner waited patiently to be cooked, wondering if on this occasion they might receive a charred outcome, or what I describe as *"well done."* It won't be long before *SpongeBob* and *Dora* episodes will end, and the children will hand me a list tied with a blue ribbon with their needs, wants, and desires—mostly wants and desires. The writer in me wanted to pack away pen and paper, or in this case the computer, and go on a writing retreat.

The caller was Eman Jajonie-Daman, an attorney and magistrate at the 46th District Court. She said there were French reporters / filmmakers in town doing a web documentary entitled *My Beloved Enemy: Iraqi American Stories*. They hoped I could introduce them to Warina Zaya Bashou who at 111 years old became the second oldest person to be granted a US citizenship. I had interviewed Warina the year prior, on January 17, 2012, for an article that was published by *The Chaldean News*. She had received nationwide media attention.

Warina lived only a few blocks from me. When I arrived to her house at eight o'clock on that cloudy and cold night in January, I was greeted by her daughter, Mary, and grand-daughter, Dina. Their spouses were there as well, as was Mary's brother-in-law, Saad. Saad had taken Warina for her citizenship test. The three women—Warina, Mary, and Dina—lived together, with a baby on the way.

Warina sat on her favorite blue camping chair, her wrinkly face and blue-eyes (though she claimed they were not blue) glowing with bliss. With her red-henna hair, colored at the recommendation of an Iraqi doctor who told her that henna remedies head pain, her blue sequenced custom-made gown, and a pale blue headscarf that tied around her forehead, she looked not a day over ninety.

Due to her hearing problem, it was oftentimes difficult to translate and so her relatives spoke on her behalf. It was even more difficult to transfer and transport her, I was told. Her fragile body and inability to walk made getting her from the house to the car, for instance, a laborious task that required some forty-five minutes. Most importantly, the family was proud to have Warina's name go down in history, which they described as "a beautiful thing for our children and their children and their children's children."

Warina said that the keys to living a long life are work, drinking tea, and not going to see the doctor. Her smile never leaving her face, she then demonstrated how in her birthplace, the village of Tel Keppe, she separated grains by shaking a sieve. She excitedly expressed that, in the village, there was a lot of love, for God, for the family, and there were very good relations. She felt very sorry for what was happening to Iraq and missed the village, the old days, and her friends. Yet she'd wanted to come to the United States to reunite with her daughter. She liked the new country and assimilated easily because everyone stood behind her.

"Who doesn't like America?" asked Saad. "It's the best

country in the world. I mean, where do you see a judge come to someone's home to swear them in?" The office of U.S. Citizenship and Immigration Services brings the swearing-in ceremony to the homes of people who have health issues that make it difficult to walk, hear, or see.

It was Saad's wife, Pam, a full-fledged American, who translated into Chaldean for Warina when the district judge read her the oath. Later, I asked how she learned Chaldean, a dialect of modern Aramaic which Chaldeans refer to as Sureth, Chaldean, or Aramaic. She said, "My mother-in-law lived with us during the first sixteen years of our marriage. My husband was mostly at work so when you have two women alone in the house, they must find a way to communicate. That's how I learned Chaldean."

The one advice Warina always gave her children was to love their parents and to not push them to the curb. "That's how it was back home," she said, adding that while she was pleased about the press attention she received (her family said she even had fun posing for the cameras while proudly holding up her naturalization paper), the real joy will be "up in heaven," she said, pointing to the sky. Her family responded, "Hopefully, she'll live another one hundred years."

At the request of Eman, the attorney, I called to see if Warina could be interviewed by the French filmmakers. Her family said she had passed away last year. The news saddened me and reaffirmed the reality of one day my mother dying and me never seeing her again. I quickly shelved the idea away as, given my mother's deteriorating health, it was too much to bear. Eman asked permission to give the filmmakers my phone number so I could assist them in finding another subject. I agreed, and shortly afterward, I received a call from a woman with a French accent. She greeted me and then explained, "We are looking for an elderly person who has received a US citizenship."

"I know many people and I can try to think of someone for you," I said. "Why don't you come over for brunch in the afternoon and we'll talk about it?"

"Oh, that would be lovely! Thank you so much."

The guttural "R" sounds, along with the skipping of so many syllables, reminded me of my love for France that began in 1999 when a friend and I hopped on a train and traveled from London to Paris for a day. The moment we landed in Paris, we knew we'd made a mistake. Paris deserved a week, a month, a year of exploration. The city was alive with the melody of cars and trucks on the streets, the colors of fashionable women, the scenery, and the Eiffel Tower. Obviously, one needed money to enjoy the endless possibilities of museums, theaters, restaurants, and shops, so I was determined to return some day and stay a lot longer.

Circumstances however didn't allow for a follow-up trip. With the help of our husbands, my friend and I made human beings, built in our wombs, and our love for them changed every atom of our being. The sense of responsibility caused us to become "Crazy Middle-Eastern Moms" who are overbearing and anxious and whatever other descriptions apply to mothers who have cultural roots in the Mediterranean such as Italians and Jews. Some stereotypes are simply true.

I tried to swap the France experience with movies and books: watched *Julie and Julia* and *Midnight in Paris* umpteen times; listened to *My Life in Paris* in the car; bought a planner with a cover photo of the Eiffel Tower. And now France, or its real-life people which were possibly Parisians, was visiting me. I needed to find a subject, quick, to secure the success of this visit.

My mother came to mind. She had a lot of similarities

to Warina; she married at age twelve, or as she always liked to emphasize, "twelve-and-a-half"; she was illiterate and attained a citizenship without knowing how to speak English; she thwarted off any idea of having another man after the death of her husband. When Warina's relatives teased about matching her up with a new husband, now that she was famous and getting media attention, she said passionately, "I'll bury him! Me, replace the father of my children!" and she swayed her arms left to right, a Chaldean way of gesturing that an idea is taboo. Both women had a true marriage of the soul. They knew who they were.

I called my sister-in-law. "Tell Mom to dress nice and to find her citizenship paper. I'm picking her up in fifteen minutes."

Before I got married, I lived with my mother, brother, his wife, and two children. Leaving to my new home saddened my mom. She continued to live with her son and his family, but I knew it didn't feel the same without me. I was thirty-four years old, and aside from when I traveled, I had always lived with her. Since she did not speak English, read, write, or drive, she relied heavily on me and my sisters, and we all played various roles in ensuring to take care of her. I drove her to most of her doctors' appointments, and when she had surgery or other more serious health issues, I stayed the night with her at the hospital.

My sister-in-law often dropped her off at my house, which was only a mile away from theirs, and we'd have lunch or dinner together, drink tea, reminisce about old times, gossip a little, and regurgitate complaints and current problems. At those times, I usually gathered my sisters too, knowing Mom loved having her children around, and they, especially her daughters, loved being around her. Their presence also spared me from engaging too closely in the gossip and complaints. Instead, I became an observer, as if watching one of Bravo's Housewives series: *Did you see how she bolted outside like a horse, dialed her boyfriend's number and had him pick her up from the street before anyone could catch up with her to drag her home? Did you notice how tiny the portions of food she served for her guests, and to top it off, she eyed that food as if it was gold! Did you hear how, while his wife was in the shower, he saw pictures on her phone of her sitting on his cousin's lap?*

Initially I detached from these "gossip" sessions as I did the dishes, laundry, cooked, or whatever other activity helped me check off my to-do list before the day ended. I was behaving like the timid or conceited girl who stood on the side and watched everyone enjoy themselves on the dance floor. But after a couple cups of coffee, I usually let my hair down, took off my house sandals, and joined the party barefoot as I engaged in these stories that were *true*! Which raises the question: Was this even gossip? Could a more accurate term be *venting* or *storytelling*? According to a recent study by Stanford scholars, while gossip and ostracism get a bad rap, they may be quite good for society and have very positive effects. They are tools by which groups reform bullies, thwart exploitation of "nice people" and encourage cooperation. Something the women in my family knew without seeking academic validation.

My mother couldn't find her original citizenship, only a copy of it, a black and white copy, reduced in quality, absent of vibrant colors, and protected by the fortress of a Ziploc bag. "This will do," I said, scanning her clothes. The knitted mauve sweater was nice, but the collar of the blue striped shirt underneath showed. The shiny brown velvet pants did not match. I asked if she had something else to wear, and she looked down and replied, "Why? What's wrong with this?"

"Nothing," I said, as time was running out and I still had to pick up pasties, get my house in order, and look half-decent before the unexpected French guests arrived.

Claire Jeantet had the typical features of French women; tall, thin, blonde, gentle, cool and collected. Accompanying her were Fabrice Catrini, the co-director, who could have passed for Claire's family member, and Thomas Bernardi, the cameraman, an Italian, I presumed. We chitchatted, each of us with our unique accents, as we enjoyed a little brunch—date syrup and sesame purée, along with other Iraqi specialties. Claire asked if I knew the status of the museum being built by the Chaldean Cultural Center (CCC) and housed inside Shenandoah Country Club. The film crew had gone there a few days prior but a man at the door did not permit them entrance, explaining it was under construction. She was disappointed, to say the least, and wondered why he hadn't let them inside, given they were visitors, filmmakers to top it off, from another country. "And from France!" I emphasized.

I didn't know the answer to her wonderment. Rumors had been spreading, piling up actually, to why it was taking eons, nine years to be exact, to build a 2,500 square foot museum in a 95,000 square foot country club located in the city of West Bloomfield. Surely, the initial $5 million budget should make the process a piece of cake. How did they plan to stuff over five thousand years of Mesopotamian history into such a small little space? And it was obvious that by placing the museum inside a country club which had one of Michigan's largest ballrooms, at 11,336 square feet, they were catering to the wealthy Chaldeans, known as "The

West-Siders"—a confusing term, in my opinion, unless someone could clearly define where the east ended and the west began. What I also didn't know was that this mysterious museum would become a big part of my life six years later.

Once we completed our brunch, we moved to the living room. My mother sat on the couch. My children frolicked from room to room. The interview began.

"Why did you want to get your citizenship?" Claire asked.

"I wanted to be like my children," my mother said, and I interpreted. "They all got their citizenship, and so it was now my turn."

My mother attained her citizenship in 1997, a tremendous accomplishment for her having never gone to school. The only schooling she received was when, in 1978, Saddam Hussein passed law number ninety-two, a literacy program that made going to school a legal obligation for every illiterate person between ages fifteen and forty-five. Anyone who refused to learn reading, writing, and arithmetic had to pay a fine of $30 or serve one week in jail. Those who lied or attempted to impede the implementation of the literacy campaign received larger fines and longer jail time.

According to a 1979 *Washington Post* article written by Edward Cody, the Iraqi government estimated it was spending nearly $200 million on the thirty-five-month program. More than two million Iraqis were said to study in 28,725 literacy schools staffed by more than 75,000 teachers. Khalid Shukri Shawkat, then the undersecretary for literacy affairs in the Education Ministry, formed "the Pioneers," a group that consisted of volunteer teachers. Classes were usually held in schools and mosques after the children had gone home and most men had ended their workday. Other classes were tailored to accommodate the community they served. The Bedouins, for instance, were assigned teachers dressed in traditional headcloth and long tunics who rode camels with their students as they went from camp to camp. Sailors had teachers join them during sea trips and provide classes there. Truck drivers and fishermen were given taped lessons so they could study on the job. Iraqi television broadcasted literacy lessons every night except Friday, the Muslim day of rest.

Some questioned the value of this type of forced learning, done mostly by memorizing, amongst people who traditionally shared stories, composed poetry, and taught life lessons via oral communication. How sincere could a student be when he or she attended class simply to avoid fines and prison terms?

Shawkat reported various complaints from students; one man missed a business opportunity because of the classes; café owners said the classes had turned into gossip sessions; the Baath Party's ideology was mixed into the lessons. Shawkat wrote, "The Ministry of Education was keen to prepare curricula in a way that ensures disseminating national education and appropriate information on the Arab homeland, especially on its leaders, geography, and history. It also concentrated on the Zionist settlement occupation in Palestine as an existing danger threating the masses' future. The ministry also aimed at educating the citizen with a unionist and socialist education."

Nevertheless, the program taught countless Iraqi men and women to read and write, something they most likely wouldn't have done on their own. This resulted in the United Nations Educational, Scientific and Cultural

Organization awarding Iraq a prize for the most effective literacy campaign in the world.

My mother attended these classes long enough to learn how to spell part of her long first name, Shamamta, and for abbreviation purposes she only used the letters *sheen* "sh" and *meem* "m." Shortly afterward, she left for Jordan to await a visa to the United States.

It seems that I helped my mother study one hundred civic test questions, not the fifty I previously thought, for her naturalization interview. Either my memory failed me, or maybe I couldn't imagine her memorizing the answers to that many questions that dealt with U.S. history, government, and the legal system. She had to get six out of ten questions right. She only got one wrong answer. I was her interpreter. Some applicants are exempt from the English language requirements when applying for US Citizenship. Applicants over the age of fifty-five with a valid Green Card who have lived in the US for fifteen years, as was her case, could take the civics test in their native language if they do not understand spoken English and must bring an interpreter to the interview.

The Oath of Allegiance to the United States is a sworn declaration that every citizenship applicant must recite during a formal ceremony in order to become a naturalized American citizen. That day, I was in a hurry to go to work. My mother wanted to take a picture with the judge, like other people had lined up to do. Occupied with a dozen responsibilities and millions of thoughts, I did not see the point of the picture. Besides, I had not taken a picture with the judge when I received my citizenship. We left the building with her request unfulfilled, and ever since, I wished I had reacted differently. I did not realize it then, but this was my mother's first major accomplishment outside of her home. She was proud to have received a document that honored her efforts, a reward, something that validated she had capabilities other than being a good housewife and mother.

"Now she got more than that picture that she had wanted sixteen years ago," I said to Claire, and we both laughed.

The recognition my mother was seeking sought her, magnified. Five months later, in September, the filmmakers showed the documentary at Visa pour L'Image, the premiere International Festival held in Perpignan, France.

"Oh Weam, your mother up there on the screen made a real impact," Claire told me through Skype. "The audience loved and applauded her."

Her words further illuminated what I had begun to understand about my mother, now that I myself was a wife and mother. This woman had deep tribal and ancestral powers that few people understood. She had impacted not only the lives of her twelve children and nearly two dozen grandchildren, but her story had landed in France and later traveled the world through the internet.

That same year, at age eighty, my mother's health drastically deteriorated. On several occasions, my siblings and I thought we were going to lose her. Later, we were also faced with the difficult choice of who would care for her now that she was in a wheelchair and had dementia. In the end, I offered to take her into my home. The process taught me quite a bit about God, life, and humanity.

My mother and I were as different as apples and oranges. She was born to farmers and raised in Tel Keppe, a once-Christian village, and she did not go to school, although she wished she had. I was born to a highly educated father in the Muslim city of Baghdad and my attendance of school was as natural as learning jumping jacks. She married my father at age twelve-and-a-half. I married my husband at thirty-four. She never went anywhere alone and rarely left her home. I traveled the world alone. From a young age, I knew I had inherited my love for words, books, education, and adventure from my father. It wasn't until later in life that I learned I could not have made my dreams come true without witnessing my mother's self-discipline, her ability to rely on her intuition and common sense, and her faith in a higher power.

Claire and I stayed in touch. She regretted not having seen the Chaldean Museum. I ended up entering into a marriage with the place.

CHAPTER 2

MUSINGS FROM LITTLE BAGHDAD

The snow accumulated on the ground that cold morning whereas the day before it was warm and sunny. The fluctuating weather in Michigan did not exist in my birth country, a land famous for its desert sands, where summer lasts nearly all year long. I turned into the parking lot of the Middle Eastern produce market. With the exception of a group of seagulls and a few cars, the area was empty.

Upon opening the entrance door, the aroma of *samoon*, Iraqi diamond-shaped bread, and a song by the Lebanese singer Fairuz took me to my childhood in Baghdad, a city once known long, long ago, as the center of learning and commerce where the House of Wisdom was built. Imagine that! The House of Wisdom was a key institution in the translation movement where Greek, Persian, Sanskrit, Chinese and Syriac works were translated into Arabic and the concept of the library catalog was introduced. When the Mongols invaded Iraq in 1258, they destroyed the House of Wisdom along with all the other libraries in Baghdad—the story of Iraq's life.

They say love kills time.
They also say time kills love.
My love, let's leave
before time and before love.

Fairuz's voice and music carried me to the days when we

lived in the district off Al Harthiya and my parents and siblings listened to her and other popular Arabic singers on the radio during the mornings, evenings, and nights. I often missed the wonderful magic I experienced when, as a child, I walked to school in a custom-made uniform, my hair in braids, tied by bright white imitation silk ribbons. I remembered those walks so well: the frosty grass in the winter, birds chirping in spring, the sounds of my shoes click-clacking against an ancient surface that once was famed as the wealthiest and richest city in the world.

I stood in front of the *tanoor* oven that was in wide view so patrons got to watch the baker place a huge wooden spatula in and out of the fire to make fresh bread. I desired to nail a bench to the ground and sit there for hours on end, watching the tanoor, the luminous fire, and thinking about days long gone, of a land I could not easily return to because of all of its political, social, and religious turmoil. It was especially not safe for me, a Christian woman, to visit my birth country where half-a-dozen years ago, my parents' and grand-parents' Christian villages were destroyed by invaders yet again. My ancient Chaldean ancestors helped build the cradle of civilization, the area presumably the location of the Garden of Eden, but over a period of thousands of years it has on-and-off been turned into a hell on earth.

Separating myself from Baghdad's memories, I walked down the flour-dusted aisles, among jars of grape leaves, olives, and tahini. I packed into the shopping cart tomatoes, English cucumbers, jalapeño peppers, clotted cream, and packaged chocolate croissants. I brought the items to the register counter and set them near the tray of freshly made *falafel* and the meat, vegetable, and cheese pasties.

The cashier greeted me, as she did all her female customers, in endearing Arabic or Aramaic terms of *love* or *dear*. She was a husky woman with a pretty face and a warm smile. She always wore black. "How much are the cauliflowers?" I asked, wanting to make pickled cabbage and cauliflower.

"One dollar each."

She began to weigh and bag my items while I went to grab five cauliflowers. As I approached the counter, she said, "You are one of very few customers who never gave us a hard time, and that's why I'm about to tell you this. Today is our last day here. We're closing the store tomorrow."

We looked at each other. I dropped one of the cauliflowers and picked it up hoping the impact hadn't crushed any of the florets. Under normal circumstances, I would've exchanged the cauliflower for an un-dropped one, but this situation called for sympathy for the woman and less concern about a possibly dented floret.

"They refuse to renew our lease," she said. "We opened this store fourteen years ago and it took us two years to fill it with groceries."

She told me her story. She'd been working since the age of twelve, and now in her forties, she'd had less than four months' time of rest altogether, including maternity leave for her two children. Her children are delighted that from now on, she'll be home when they return from school. Her husband had wanted her to stop working so they could spend more time together and go to church on Sundays. But her sister, who owned the store with their brother and her husband, needed her there. Their father having passed away when they were young, the two sisters had worked side-by-side since their teenage years.

"My mother pushed us to work," she said. "Even now, she says that after the store closes, I should find a job. My husband is well-off and I don't really need to work."

I told her that I too started working at age twelve, with my mother prodding me to work, work, and work. And like her, I too was sad when we closed a family video store I'd managed for twelve years. I worked there seven days a week and knew all the customers. But in my case, after I had children, I did not work out of the home. My husband and I made a number of sacrifices for this lifestyle.

We chitchatted a little more, she expressing her grief, hopes, and dreams, and me giving her words of advice and encouragement. We wished each other the best of luck and I walked out, the essence of the past trailing behind me like a long wedding veil. I walked into the snow, into my city, nicknamed "Little Baghdad" because of the large population of Iraqi Americans primarily of the Christian faith, largely Chaldeans and Assyrians. At almost every corner is a Middle Eastern produce market, restaurant, bakery, butcher shop, and hookah lounge, some with Arabic signate: Baghdad Market, Sahara Restaurant, Ishtar Restaurant, Babylon Fruit Market, Chickpea Kitchen, Pacha Al Mosul, and the list goes on. Inside the stores, outside of the schools, during walks, and practically everywhere else, I hear the Aramaic dialect between men and women who, like my family, left our ancestors' land for freedom and a better life.

As an immigrant, I've often felt that I had one foot in one world and the other foot in another, with a gap in between. Sometimes that gap narrowed to the point of closure, and other times it opened wider and wider, becoming as wide as a shark's jaws—a tiger not angel shark. When I was a child, I'd spent years wanting to ask my family, "Why did you uproot me from my birthplace?" I felt like a plant taken out of its soil. Plants often enter a state of shock as they adapt to the new environment and struggle to get over the abruptness of being uprooted and repotted.

We left Iraq in 1980, missing the Iraq-Iran war by an inch. The day we left was so hush-hush, I didn't even know about it. One day I was in Baghdad, and the next day, *poof!*, I was in Jordan. I have no recollection of our actual departure. We disappeared as quickly as sugar in a cup of hot tea, and then we began a new life. We lived in Amman, Jordan, for nearly a year as we awaited our visas. Because we were nonresidents in Jordan, my younger brother and I were not permitted to enroll in school. We spent 90 percent of our time indoors, watching *Scooby-Doo*, *Little House on the Prairie*, and *Charlie's Angels*, and playing house with the Mahjong bone bamboo set that my sister's Japanese boss gave her. We used the tiles carved with colorful and pretty Chinese symbols, including flowers, to build houses, furniture, staircases, as dolls, etc. The flowers on the tiles represented the four Confucian plants: bamboo (summer), chrysanthemum (autumn), orchid (spring), and plum (winter). They are known as the Four Gentlemen of China.

We finally set foot on Michigan soil on February 2, 1981, and I was introduced to the real version of America. Until the plane landed at Detroit Metropolitan Airport, I thought that America was merely a story. In Baghdad, the word "America" was like a powerful perfume capturing people's senses, creating an overwhelming surge of emotion that transported you to another place and time. That word entered our home the moment the Baath party came into power in 1968, and apparently my father decided to pack up his family and move out of Iraq. He wanted us to have political and religious freedom as Christians.

Iraqis of all sects were forced to join the Baath Party to secure good jobs or promotions and even enter universities. In order to have some rights, many people paid the membership fees but were not active Baathists. In addition, Christians, like Jews and other minorities, were considered second class citizens, even though they were in their own homeland. They too did not receive the same job and promotion opportunities.

Exceptions were made for very intelligent and resourceful men and women such as my father who was the head of the accounting department for the railroad station. Saddam Hussein, who served as Iraq's fifth president from 1979 to 2003, did not see Christians as a threat and therefore appointed Tariq Aziz, a Chaldean, as his prime minister. That's why he treated them decently in comparison to other rulers, especially those who followed his presidency. But in general, as Christian non-Baathists, we had two points against us.

Those who didn't join the Baath Party, like my father, were ostracized. In the early 1970s, when my father expressed certain political views, his boss, who was a Baathist, gave him notice to leave our government-owned house. My father, who had a wife and nine of his eleven children to take care of (two of his daughters were already married), didn't comply, so they cut off our electricity and water for a month, forcing us to leave. They then demoted him by relocating him to Samawah, nearly 175 miles southeast of Baghdad. Not having a car to drive the three hours each way, he visited us by train weekly, sometimes biweekly. All this broke my father's heart.

My oldest brother was the first to leave and immigrate to the United States in the 1970s. Once there, he petitioned for the rest of us to join him, apart from the married sisters who were not considered "eligible relatives" by INS (Immigration and Naturalization Service). It was a drawn-out process and during that time, my siblings worked hard, saved up money, and sent it to him and his wife so they could establish a home and business for everyone else once we arrived in the new country. One of my sisters came first to America as a nanny for my brother, by then married with two children, and later my father followed.

When we arrived, I remember it was a cold, sunny day with light snow. While the RV that picked up our family of eight from the airport drove on the highway, I, a ten-year-old, watched the snow and the empty streets through the window. It seemed vacant—no one was walking, riding a bike, pushing a baby stroller, or sitting on a front porch. The highlight of our ride was the eighty-foot, twelve-ton Uniroyal Giant Tire next to Interstate 94 (I-94) near the airport.

"This is a landmark," said my Americanized brother. "When you see this tire, you know that you're in Detroit."

My brother's brother-in-law, one of the older American settlers in the RV, told us the story of how this tire was once a Ferris wheel for the 1964-1965 World Fair in New York. It was built by the same company that built the Empire State Building, and some of the millions of people who rode it were Jackie Kennedy and the Shah of Iran. When the fair closed in 1965, the Ferris wheel was disassembled and shipped to Detroit. It took four months to put it back together near I-94.

The giant tire was interesting, but where was the excitement that we saw on television? The crowded, congested streets? The taxis and buses, the food stands, the pigeons in the park, the people walking dogs? One of the new arrivals in the van expressed this discrepancy. "That's in New York," one of the older settlers explained. "We're in Michigan, a totally different state."

We then received our first unofficial course on the United States. The United States comprises of 50 states, and some are so different than one another that when you travel there, you think you're in a different country. Chaldeans began to immigrate to the United States in the early twentieth century. The majority settled in metropolitan Detroit because of its growing automobile industry. Detroit also had an established Middle Eastern community that consisted primarily of Christian Lebanese immigrants. While these communities did not speak Aramaic, Chaldeans spoke Arabic and were therefore able to communicate with them. Once Chaldeans settled in the area and prospered, they encouraged others from their homeland to join them.

I, myself, had not expected Michigan to look like New York. I'd expected it to look like Scarlett O'Hara's Tara, a fictional plantation near Atlanta, Georgia, featured in *Gone with the Wind*. Since my younger brother and I weren't able to go to school in Amman, I, at age nine, read my first novel, *Gone with the Wind*, in Arabic. I immediately connected with Scarlett's southern charm and her tribe, which in many ways resembled mine. That novel gave me the impression that American women wore huge puffy dresses, said "sir" and "madam," had extravagant barbecues broken up by extravagant naps, and were waited on hand and foot by servants. Seeing how enthralled I was with the novel, my siblings took me to a movie theater for the first time to watch *Gone with the Wind* with Arabic subtitles.

But Michigan in the 1980s was not Georgia in the 1860s, and Shelby Township, where we first lived, was not Tara. I lay in my bunk bed that first night with my face pressed against the wall, the pillows absorbing a cupful of tears. Reality finally set in. I would never again live in the neighborhood where I grew up. I was no longer going to see my friends. We never even said goodbye.

I wanted to ask my family, "Why did you uproot me from my birthplace?" But they were so busy acclimating and surviving, I could not express how I felt. For a long time, I struggled to fit into two worlds—my birth country of Iraq and my new home, America. The process made me feel like a yo-yo and, oftentimes, as if I were living a double life. It was especially di-cult when I had to witness the various American wars in Iraq.

I pulled into our driveway and brought the groceries in through the garage door. The house was lulled into a slumber with my children off to school, my husband at work, and my mother still sleeping. I put away the groceries, went into her room, and saw her staring at the ceiling.

"*Sabah al khair,*" I greeted her with morning blessings.

"*Sabah al khair,*" she replied in Arabic and added *welcome* in Aramaic, "*Halla ib gawakh.*"

I began the ritual of transporting her into her wheelchair, taking her to the lavatory, changing and grooming her, then wheeling her chair to the kitchen table where I prepared a breakfast of sliced Spanish cheese, watermelon and pita bread. Once she finished her breakfast, I brought her to the living room and turned on the Arabic Satellite TV, the movie channel that played the Egyptian classics we grew up on, which most of the Arab World loved, and still loves.

As I went about my day, writing, cleaning, and cooking Iraqi meals, she and I both traveled to the memories we had in our younger days. We were happy. We'd arrived at a place in our lives where she'd completely surrendered to who she was, and I no longer had the burning question to ask her, "Why did you uproot me from my birthplace?" Once I became a mother, I began to understand and appreciate my parents' decisions. I realized that home is the atmosphere you create, and identity is partly your dream and partly someone else's dream of you.

CHAPTER 3

CHALDEAN TOWN

"Little Baghdad" ought to be called "Chaldean Town," a name already given to a Detroit neighborhood around Seven Mile Road, which stretches east from Woodward Avenue to John R. Road. That area was a first stop for many Chaldeans who began emigrating to the United States in the 1920s. Back then, they bought houses, opened businesses on the main strip and created a flourishing neighborhood of restaurants and shops with a Middle Eastern essence. They settled in the Penrose neighborhood, where some streets had homes so old, they didn't have driveways because they were built before cars were invented. There was barely space to walk between them.

The Detroit area was declared Chaldean Town in 1999, although today you won't find many Chaldeans there, if any. The city had the idea to curb the decline by investing and promoting the neighborhood. They came up with the name Chaldean Town to mark it as a destination—like a Middle Eastern version of the long-successful Greektown. There would be colorful banners hanging from light posts, declaring the area's name. An annual ethnic festival on Seven Mile Road would close the street to traffic. A Chaldean Town Development Authority would oversee the neighborhood's progress. But like a lot of plans in Detroit, the grants never came, the idea faded away, and the strip continued its free fall.

My family never lived in "Seven Mile," the name people

gave that region, but I had two friends who did: Norma, a Jordanian/Palestinian whom I met in high school, and Rita, a Chaldean whose parents lived in Iraq with my parents in what was called a *mujtamal*, a house separated by a courtyard and shared by a number of families. Norma lived on Brentwood Street, and in my late teens, early twenties, I'd often visit her home. When we weren't in her room chatting and drinking tea, we'd sit on the porch and watch the Chaldean men pass by in their fancy cars, rap music blasting. They'd flirt with us using various car techniques: lowering or raising the volume of the music, squealing their tires, bouncing the car by pumping the brakes, or playing songs aimed at our affections. Stevie B's *Spring Love* was an all-time favorite.

Don't you know I'm the one and I love you girl.
I don't care what they say you know you are my world.

Amr Diab's *My Life* was a new release used by men who tried to get their girl back after a breakup, or situations where the girl played extremely hard to get:

Oh my life, my heart, who do I have but you?
Who do I have but you?
I'm tired and worn out,
I'm tired and worn out
being far away from you.

Of course, there were always the sassier guys who only cared about a girl's physical attributes and would blast Sir Mix-a-Lot's lyrics "I like big butts and I cannot lie, you other brothers can't deny" as they passed by, maybe even shouting from their topless cars, "…when a girl walks in with an itty-bitty waist, and a round thing in your face, you get sprung!"

Norma and I would act offended, but once they were gone, we'd laugh and tease each other about all the attention. I'd always leave her house before dark, when the neighborhood's social scene was replaced by empty streets, locked doors, and the occasional sounds of gun shots.

The uninhibited hormonal experience at Norma's Street took place in the early 1990s. During the mid-to-late 1980s is when I mostly visited Rita's house. Rita lived on Charleston Street, which her mother often described as "Church Street" since Goodwill Community Chapel was located on the corner right on Seven Mile Road and Charleston Street. A few buildings down from the chapel was Sacred Heart Chaldean Catholic Church, converted from a store to a church. Established in 1973 by Reverend Jacob Yasso, the building was later altered to resemble the Gate of Ishtar in Ancient Babylon. Its name, Sacred Heart, is the name of one of the two churches originally located in the village of Telkaif. One newspaper article describes the building as a squat wooden church that "juts out like an overgrown shed on a street of abandoned shops."

The church's famous story is that, in 1979, it received a check for $250,000 from Saddam Hussein after its priest, Father Yasso, congratulated Saddam on his new presidency. Later, Father Yasso went to Baghdad, told Saddam of his church's debt, and got another $200,000. This helped pay off the bank loan and build the Chaldean Educational Center of America [CECA] next door to the church. As a result, Mayor Coleman Young awarded Saddam the key to the city of Detroit.

I visited Rita's house with my family because I didn't yet have a driver's license. Not long after I got my driver's license she married and moved to Australia. So I didn't spend as much time with her sitting on the front porch, a pastime her father disapproved of anyway. We mostly talked on the phone. Her home was full of visitors and her kitchen always had large pots of food that could feed a small army. Her mother would place some of the plentiful food into several Tupperware on the front porch for the homeless people who came and picked them up.

As the years passed by, Norma, Rita, and I led our separate lives, got married and had children, and the neighborhoods in Seven Mile greatly deteriorated. The crack epidemic and crime ravaged the neighborhood and made the schools more dangerous, with the sound of gunfire at night increasing. Chaldeans began to move to the suburbs, having learned "back home" that, that's what you do when you feel you or your family is in harm's way. Their departure left a stretch of abandoned buildings and burnt homes.

After over a decade of not having been there, I drove to Seven Mile on Tuesday, April 14 of 2009 to do a story on Chaldean Town for *The Chaldean News*. The editor-in-chief thought I would be good for this article since many Chaldeans in that area did not speak English. I was to give a feel for the neighborhood as it is now compared to the past, and an idea of its future. Will the church be able to continue? What was being done for the Chaldean community there?

The nonprofit Arab American and Chaldean Council (ACC) was one of five organizations trying to restore Seven Mile, to make it a more friendly and safe environment where people didn't fear that someone could just walk into your home and kill you, where dogs didn't roam outside without their owners, fires weren't set to burn homes, and where the summer heat was not combatted by air-conditioners. Basically, a place that didn't look like Iraq or any other warzone.

I arrived to the church's door that resembled the Ishtar Gate. At seven months pregnant, I carried in my belly the next generation, a child I knew not yet the gender of, a child which one day, perhaps, would grow up to probe into its lineage and discover its significance. I stood there, centered by the love of family, community, and tradition, and simultaneously possessed and intrigued by the power of individuality and unconventionality; balancing the two worlds as they sit on opposite sides of a seesaw.

I stood there wondering what to expect from Father Yasso, a man in his mid-seventies known to wear a black beret with his long black garment. He had been somewhat upset when I called him to schedule our meeting. I imagined his arched eyebrows as he said in a suspicious voice that *The Chaldean News* had interviewed him twice before but the articles were never published. At first, he even refused to be interviewed, but then he cooled off and said I could visit the church after Easter. *The Chaldean News* denied his accusations, said it was rare they covered a story that didn't go to print, and implied that some individuals in certain professions tended to give them a hard time.

Father Yasso and I sat on chairs facing each other, both a bit overweight for different purposes. He was handsome and healthy-looking with receding gray hair and good teeth, or dentures. He had on a sweater with colorful zig-zag patterns over a grey shirt that showed his clerical collar.

"There are less than 150 Chaldean families left here," he told me, with a small and pleasant smile that carried over seven decades of memories. His voice echoed inside the silence of the large church. "Many have left the neighborhood for the suburbs."

Those who attended Sunday mass, including the deacons, were primarily out-of-towners who lived in nearby cities. The last time children received First Communion at Sacred Heart Chaldean Church was in 2005. This was quite a change since the late 70's, early 80's, when two thirds of the Seven Mile community was Chaldean.

"The violence that occurred afterward had a lot to do with people moving out," Father Yasso said, recalling the rampant drug dealing and murders, one of which was a Chaldean bride and groom who were shot to death the morning of their wedding day.

Despite the deterioration in the number of Chaldean households, Father Yasso loved his parish and was determined to keep it active. He still had his house there and held parties and plays at the Chaldean Educational Center of America across the street from the church.

"My love is for these people—the poor people," he said. "I call myself the millionaire of Seven Mile, because when people come here for help, I do all I can to meet their needs."

The street adjacent to Sacred Heart Church was filled with beautiful homes that were adorned with religious objects. I viewed the church from the outside as I drove away, entering the world that was racing on in swift speed. For most of us, there were always things to do, places to go, people to see, and yet, in his old age and familiar environment, Father Yasso had the freedom to stand and stare.

I arrived to Almost 99 Cent store to meet Raad Sawa, its owner. His business was greatly affected by the neighborhood's vacancy and the economy. He pointed out that the only decent neighborhood street on Seven Mile was the one adjacent to the church. The rest were filled with abandoned or burnt houses and garbage.

"If the city fixes the houses, then people will come," he said.

Raad attended a meeting a few days prior at the ACC's Youth Recreation and Leadership Center, where Mayor Kenneth Cockrel Jr. assured members of the Arab American and Chaldean Council (ACC) that his administration backed revitalization efforts in the Seven Mile area. The mayor encouraged people to tell him which buildings and houses were abandoned so that his administration could quickly identify "trouble spots."

"ACC's and the mayor's ideas are good, but they take a long time," Raad said. "They have to move quick."

"What about the substantial decrease in crime and violence and the improvements that occurred on Seven Mile?" I asked, reviewing my notes: According to statistics, homicide in Detroit went down from 392 in 2007 to 323 in 2008; the revitalization strategies for the Seven Mile corridor and nearby neighborhoods were clearly underway. "There's also the renovations of major buildings, cleanliness, and the trees and benches."

"Yes, the streets look beautiful, but for what? We need people brought here. We also need security."

After interviewing Mr. Sawa, I returned to my car and drove to ACC to speak with the director of the Seven Mile project, Isa Hasan. He admitted that Seven Mile had become a dumping ground and insisted they were going to change that. They had made a lot of improvements, he said, adding, "We've put a stop to the bleeding of businesses closing here."

In 2005, the ACC opened its doors to a free after-school youth program providing more than three hundred kids with homework assistance, academic tutoring, life skills, service learning, computer skills, leadership, health education, and conflict resolution, along with physical programs such as basketball, dance and hands-on activities. There was always a police officer on hand. Isa said that he had not only received a commitment from the mayor to prevent police force cuts, but they are actually trying to expand by providing a foot patrol police program.

After interviewing Mr. Hasan, I returned to my car and drove to Najeeb Restaurant to speak with the owner, Najeeb Hermiz. He said that Seven Mile was neglected, that organizations like ACC send their employees only periodically to review the area's issues.

"If you don't clean your house every day, the house will rot," he said.

He and his wife complained that when they call the police, no one shows up. For safety purposes, they locked the restaurant doors as early as 7 p.m. and opened it only to their regular customers.

"The burnt homes should have been rebuilt and given to the immigrants coming through the United Nations," said Najeeb. "These immigrants who are now having financial troubles, would've afforded the low-income housing." Eventually Najeeb moved his restaurant seven miles north to Warren, a city adjacent to Sterling Heights.

Seven Mile's most loyal and happy Chaldeans at that time were those who had been living there for decades. One sixty-seven-year-old woman, Margaret, said she was often encouraged by relatives to move out. But she will never do so.

"I like it here," she said. "People here are kind, and everything is of walking distance."

Although she had encountered her own share of violence, she did not attribute it to the neighborhood but to her so-called "enemies."

Majid Yousif, the brother of my childhood friend, Rita, did not plan to move out either, even though he was the only Chaldean resident left on the street where recently, a group of teenage black boys had beaten up a Chaldean boy. Years prior, two men broke into Majid's house in the middle of the night while his parents slept. The parents were traumatized and experienced a lot of health issues afterward.

"I've been living here for over thirty years," he said, "so everyone knows me, and no one gives me trouble."

Neither of us mentioned the incident with his parents. Eventually Majid did leave his lifelong home.

I returned to my car and drove to Car Source to meet with the owner Saad Maria, my brother-in-law. His business had been on the corner of Seven Mile and John R. since 1985. He agreed that Seven Mile's major issue was security, and asked, "What's the use of a tree and bench in the street if you're afraid to sit there because someone might come and hold you up?"

Saad's business was not affected by the dwindling Chaldean population. It had even expanded. He started out with a 100ft-by-100ft lot that held only twenty-five cars. By 2009, the dealership was five times as big, with a large two-story office building and a lot that holds 250 cars.

"The majority of my customers come from other neighborhoods," he said. "And now with the internet, I even get people from out of state." He believed that a lot of Chaldeans were afraid to come to Seven Mile, even as customers. "I'm willing to pay fifty dollars a month [in taxes] to add security at night—from eight at night to early morning. If each business did that, and these jobs go to the Chaldean men who are in search of work, then we will have a safer and more prosperous community."

I left Chaldean Town before the afternoon concluded, and I headed to my mother's house for a post-Easter gathering since she had ended up in the hospital over the weekend. Our Easter was spent only with my in-laws. I felt a little sad and nostalgic seeing how the once lively Seven Mile area was replaced by an eerie emptiness. The beauty of it was gone, but the memories will always remain with me.

Twelve years later, while writing this book, I decided to look at what has happened to Chaldean Town through Google Maps. I saw that the attempts to save it had failed. Chaldean Town died, along with Father Yasso and Isa Hasan, the main people that had hope for that area. Its neighborhoods are in total blight with boarded up and burnt homes and businesses, empty streets, and a sign on the doors of Sacred Heart Church that reads "permanently closed." Goodwill Community Chapel, which opened in 1960, closed as well. Of the dozens of little businesses on the Seven Mile strip that catered to the Chaldeans and gave this area its name and ethnic flavor, only one was left. Sullaf Restaurant had no menu, and the entrees were whatever the cook made that day. Its owner, Safaa Momika, a man in his early seventies was "the last man standing," surrounded by vacant buildings that once were named Bahi, Tigris, Iraqi Bakery, and others. When editing this chapter, I learned that Sullaf Restaurant closed after its owner was diagnosed with cancer in early 2022. The once lively Seven Mile now really looks like a haunted street.

I remembered Isa's words, "We can't expect Seven Mile to flourish with the current economy crisis. I think we've seen the worst. We're on an upward climb. The Seven Mile area is more encouraging than a few years ago." Regretfully, he was wrong. All these initiatives led to nowhere. I suppose no initiative can succeed without its people stepping up to the plate and getting involved.

Once upon a time in the Seven Mile neighborhood there was a homogenous community that worked beautifully together. It consisted of people of all skin color; fair, golden, buttery, medium, olive, brown, black, caramel, cinnamon. There was a real safety net because people knew each other and watched out for each other. Today, Chaldean Town shares the fate of Poletown and several other once-vibrant ethnic Detroit neighborhoods that survive only in the memories of the suburbanites who once lived there. The inhabitants of two Chinatowns scattered to the suburbs after crime hit their communities hard in the 1970s, while New York's Chinatown continues to thrive. A historic and entertainment district that remains vibrant in Detroit is Mexicantown but Greektown, one of my favorite places, has lost its luster with much of its authentic Greekness replaced by the casino experience.

As Chaldean Town disappeared, newer Chaldean neighborhoods have appeared in other parts of Metro Detroit. Father Yasso never left. He died in his home on December 29, 2014, at age eighty-two. The buildings he established are still standing. His Facebook page is filled with posts of colored and black and white pictures: him standing in front of the Notre Dame of Paris in the early 1960s, wearing a cassock and looking quite handsome; conducting mass at the Vatican in 1960; greeting his Holiness Pope John II in the Vatican in 1985; posing with extended family; standing with clergy at the site of Sacred Heart in Detroit before construction began. Some of the more recent posts stated, "Stop the Iraqi Christian Holocaust."

The first attempt at opening a Chaldean museum occurred at Father Yasso's Chaldean Educational Center of America. That building, also shaped like the Ishtar Gate and labeled "permanently closed," still stands. Although known by its legal name, the building's sign never included the word "educational" because it was mostly used for cultural events. It has an S on one arch and an H on the other arch which stood for Sacred Heart, the church name. The initials coincidentally match the name of Saddam Hussein.

That early museum idea didn't last long and for various reasons, it moved from Chaldean Town to another location in West Bloomfield. Other members of the community pursued its development. Around the same year the construction for the museum began inside of Shenandoah Country Club, in 2007, I cofounded and was elected president of the Iraqi Artists Association (IAA), a nonprofit organization that was registered under the umbrella of CECA. This resulted in me being voted a year later as vice president of CECA. Ten years later, in 2017, the world's first and only Chaldean Museum opened its door to the public, with a celebration that included a grand reenactment of a Chaldean wedding reception.

There's a saying that "Things don't die, they become shells. Life then continues in different ways." The life in the northern villages of Iraq that were once succulent with love, warmth, safety, and food, is now a shell, it's dead, and yet it still flourishes in another physical space. Similarly, the efforts, desires, sweat, and concern that was put into Chaldean Town, later moved and was successful elsewhere. Which brings us to Sterling Heights, aka "Little Baghdad."

CHAPTER 4

MY NATIVE AMERICAN FRIEND

Ten years had passed since I'd last seen the Oneida Man. Then one afternoon in July, I called the junkyard looking for him. The answering machine came on with a woman's voice. I left a message, not knowing if he would ever receive it, if he had moved or was still alive.

A few days later, while I was organizing stuff in our basement, a number from South Carolina appeared on my phone. It was him, the Oneida Man, who I used to call Red Indian for over two decades, not realizing it was coated with controversy. It was simply the term Middle Easterners used for Native Americans.

"You live in South Carolina now?" I asked.

"No, I'm still here. My sister lives there and I got this phone when I was visiting her."

We exchanged some niceties. His voice hadn't changed—soft and flat, very matter of fact. Minutes passed before I told him I was going through my journals and came across a conversation we once had some two decades ago where he'd told me, "We want you to write about our stories." I did a little research but was not able to find stories similar to what he'd told me over the years about his tribe and other natives.

"What you're going to find is a history that is favorable. It isn't a history that's truthful," he said. "It was not healthy to be a native a few hundred years ago. People were in hiding. They felt they were being hunted."

I told him I wanted to hear the stories that I couldn't seem to find in books.

"A friend of mine, who was eighty at the time, wanted to hear stories about natives. The people who he asked, the wise people, said to him, 'Me too.'" He laughed. "He died when he was ninety years old, but the old people said to him, 'Me too.'"

I told him how I sometimes feel the energy of Native Americans around me.

"The reason you feel that energy is because at Mound Road and M59 Highway, there were burial grounds for Native Americans. Now there are buildings and townhouses and subdivisions. It's right on top of where the mounds are. That's why it's called Mound Road. That's just, for instance, native history to understand why you have certain feelings. Sterling Heights won't tell you where you are. They don't even know where you are."

I told him I wanted to learn more about his tribe and the areas where I've lived and worked since I came from Iraq to the United States almost thirty-five years ago. Who lived here and how did they live? What happened to them? Who were Ryan and Dequindre and Van Dyke, names given to the roads surrounding the city of Sterling Heights? He said I could visit the junkyard.

"It's a bit hard to find someone to watch my kids so I'd have to bring them," I said.

"Oh sure, bring them. Do your kids like cats? I have eleven kittens that were just born."

"Okay, I'll bring them."

"*Nagewa.* That means 'see you again.' That's how we end a visit."

"Nagewa," I said, and we hung up.

The day I planned to see the Oneida Man my sister-in-law called me on a sunny Sunday in August. She told me there were protests around the corner of my street. They started at St. Mary's Assyrian Church at Fourteen Mile Road and went to Seventeen Mile Road. At that corner, two groups of the protests met and then together walked back south toward Fourteen Mile Road. I got dressed and went to meet the rally as it came north toward our area. The kids were on their scooters, I walked.

"Where are we going?" my son kept asking.

I didn't know what to say. Do I tell him that we are going to a rally, explain what a rally is and why it is taking place? He's five years old. Is he supposed to hear these things, or not, and if not, when? How old does he have to be to hear the truth? Is it good to tell him or should he be left in his innocence? What about my daughter? She's eight years old. Should I explain to her that there are children being decapitated in Iraq by vicious men and we are out here to do what? Cry on their behalf? What good would that do the mother and father of the child that is decapitated?

The neighborhood was quiet, with only birds chirping and squirrels chasing each other. As soon as we stepped out of the subdivision onto the main road, Ryan Road, we heard cars honking their horns and people shouting into megaphones. "Obama, Obama, where are you? Obama, Obama, shame on you! Christian Iraqis, they need you."

American, Iraqi, Chaldean, and Assyrian flags fluttered in the air like the leaves on a tree. Most of the protesters wore white T-shirts with the words "Stop Killing Iraqi Christians" in red. Others wore white T-shirts marked with a red N in Arabic, which stood for *Nasrani,* and was the letter that the

Islamic State marked the homes of Christians in our peoples' villages of Iraq. Signs and banners depicted pictures of murdered children and demanded that the US Government end the genocide in Iraq.

"Obama, Obama, where are you?" shouted one of the protesters leading the procession into a megaphone. The crowd followed his chorus. "Obama, Obama, shame on you! Iraqi Christians need you!" Later, we heard, "Down ISIS! Save Iraqi Christians!"

As we walked closer to the crowd, the powerful aroma of kabob grabbed our attention. Several Iraqi restaurants and produce markets stood on the corner of Seventeen Mile and Ryan Road. A large barbecue grill was parked on the sidewalk, offering free hotdogs and cold bottled water to protesters. I asked who donated the food and drink, and they said, "The Ice Hookah and Tobacco Shop."

My children complained of the heat and fatigue. I assured them we would be home in five minutes, although I knew it would be longer. It was longer, closer to an hour. I had the chance to interview a few people and take down the name of the man holding the megaphone, Nabil Nona. He wore a red shirt, sunglasses, and was probably in his mid to late thirties.

On the way home, we came across two fruit trees, one growing red pears and the other green pears, which, as tradition had it, I ate from for nourishment during my afternoon walks. I plucked four green pears, poured a little water over them, rubbed them for cleanliness, gave one to each of my children, and kept two for myself.

Before turning onto our street, my son stopped at a house with a ceramic welcome sign planted in the grass and an American flag hanging from a large tree bark. He asked me to take a picture of him next to the flag. I didn't take him seriously since, for over a year, he had refused to take photos, or when forced to pose, refused to look at the camera. But when he insisted, I realized he was serious. Then I understood. He wanted to imitate the protesters who proudly raised their flags as I took their pictures.

Later that day, before taking the kids to Bible camp, we drove to the junkyard to visit the Oneida Man.

The junkyard was across the street of what once was our family's video store, which I managed for twelve years and where the Oneida Man visited me to chat. It was now an Arabic produce market. The gas station on the corner of the road was once a pasture. Next door was a gravel pit, a hole filled with water. The place was called "Bare Ass Lake" by the kids who hung out there when they skipped school and drank beer all day. The ground is solid now. After years of being filled by the previous and current owners, it became a junkyard.

I parked the minivan. We got out, walked to the office, and I asked a man for the Oneida Man.

"He's inside, just go through the back."

"Mom, there are the kittens," my daughter said.

Eleven kittens sat beside the office porch. On the way, a woman walked out of the office and took a hard look at us.

"You have new additions, I see," she said.

"Yeah." I realized that she was the Oneida Man's sister.

The junkyard was no longer a junkyard but filled with parked lorries and junk trucks. I could not see the Oneida Man anywhere. My kids were busy drinking the Slurpee and snacks I bought for them from 7-Eleven, which now occupied what used to be my eldest brother's store. It was in a plaza that he built and over the years it had various businesses, from a video store to men's tailor shop, pizzeria, dry-cleaner, and mortgage and real estate office.

"Hi there."

I'd recognize that voice anywhere. He had talked to me quite often at the video store. A man with short hair appeared, holding a metal coffee cup. His body was the same, medium height, medium built, and although he wasn't very old, he had no teeth. But as long as I had known him, the Oneida Man had long hair, usually tied in a ponytail.

"You cut your hair," I said.

He sat on one of the two plastic chairs in front of a small trailer. He didn't comment about the hair and looking around, I said, "I've never been inside this place before."

"It used to be a junkyard, but now I lease it for these lorries to park in."

Several spider mosquitos landed on my shoulder. I shooed them away. My children played in the dirt as we talked. My son kept talking about poop and booty and after some time passed my daughter came to me and said, "Mom, I'm bored."

"Mom, you're bleeding," my son said, touching my shoulder.

There was quite a bit of blood.

"That's from the spider mosquito," said the Oneida Man.

I wiped the blood with my hands and my skin turned pink. My children returned to playing and I asked him to tell me about the mounds. I had read that Mound Road is named after an Indian burial ground, now destroyed, that was discovered near that road. It is believed that the earliest settlers of the Americas were in Michigan about twelve thousand years ago. The Europeans distinguished what they called "Mound Builders" from the natives they found because they assumed the Native Americans were too culturally uncivilized to develop such large and complex structures. Since the local natives failed to explain the origins of the mounds, the Europeans reasoned that their white race or advanced societies from the

Middle East had once lived in the New World until they were annihilated by the natives.

The Oneida Man had a different take on this story.

"The reason the natives did not tell Europeans about the origins of the mounds was because, historically, we noticed that if you told the Europeans not to do something, they went ahead and did it just to see what would happen. That's their nature. So, we saw that it was better not to tell them anything because they belittled everything in America, going as far as raiding the ancient burial sites for treasures and artifacts."

Another observation the natives made was that the Europeans always wanted to know why and how, so that they could change it. "They wanted to change everything instead of taking it as it is," he said. "The reason they wanted to change everything is because they viewed what they have as real and true and everything else that others had as unreal and fictitious."

In 1894, Cyrus Thompson of the Smithsonian Institution concluded that the Mound Builders were, in fact, the Native Americans. The majority of those who built those mounds had died of diseases or had been enslaved in the decades following the Spanish exploration of the region. The mounds were built over a span of thousands of years by different types of people, ranging from hunter-gatherers to farmers. The earliest mounds in the United States were found at Watson Brake near Monroe, Louisiana, built in the late fourth millennium BC. Over a thousand mounds in Michigan have long since been flattened and turned into streets and lots.

"That's why there aren't that many Indians here," the Oneida Man told me. "There used to be lots. Now there's no *lots*."

After the war with the British, cannons were set up in Detroit, Algonac, and Port Huron so that natives who left for

Canada could not return to their land. Treaties were made, at the point of a rifle, with various Indian tribes from 1814 to 1819 freeing up much land for settlement.

On our way out, the Oneida Man pointed ahead and said, "There's a groundhog. You just missed him. We get rabbits here and deer, all kinds of animals. It's fun."

We arrived home exhausted. The next morning, I began calling the numbers I collected from people at the rally to interview them. *Why were you at the rally? How do you feel about the Islamic State destroying your ancestral villages? What do you expect the United States to do to stop this killing?* I received a lot of heartfelt answers and had the longest conversation with a man in his forties who appeared the most gung-ho about the protest. He had all the protest paraphernalia imaginable, held multiple flags, and spoke fervently and candidly. He had issues with Sterling Heights "security" being there. "We are peaceful people, they don't need to be there," he said and went on to tell me that he almost got into a fight with the flag holders (fellow protesters), told them to call the police if they wanted; almost punched someone in a protest in Washington; and got into it with the Muslim protesters denouncing ISIS.

He felt this was not the time to drum up that Islam is a religion of peace. He and many others, however, were most impressed by a beautiful *hijabi* woman in her early twenties who used the megaphone to passionately take lead in the procession and speak against the Islamic State. Swarms of Chaldeans and Assyrians approached her and thanked her for her support. Many suggested I meet her in person, so I contacted her. We had coffee together at Tim Hortons. I write about our encounter in my book *Iraqi Americans: Witnessing a Genocide*.

I kept contact with this woman until one day she posted in the middle of the night a picture on Facebook of her face badly beaten up by relatives. She quickly took down the picture, closed her Facebook account, and disappeared. She reappeared years later with a different name, account and a completely unrecognizable look without the hijab. Her new look relied heavily on dark erotica. She was openly suicidal, and on the verge of destruction. I remembered how she had fervently spoken out against injustice in Iraq, not knowing then that it was because injustice was being done to her.

Chapter 5

AN ACCIDENTAL TRIP TO THE MASJID

People took off their snow-sprinkled shoes and sandals at the door. A golden silk curtain partially separated the men from the women and children. The women, wearing colorful head scarves and *kurtis*, warmly greeted me. I asked them whether it was okay for me, as a Christian, to be here in a *masjid*. They said, "Yes, definitely. Please feel at home."

I took off my shoes, wishing I had worn my better socks on this cold January night. Although no one batted an eye, I also respectfully put my long hair in a bun. I'd visited a mosque before in London, so I wasn't a complete novice. And there once was a time when I was part of the Muslim world, and it was a part of me. I grew up hearing the *adhan*, the Islamic call to prayer, scheduled five times per day. Each time I heard it, I entered a dreamy state as the *muezzin* in the nearby mosque poetically chanted the Quran, sent out through loud speakers that seemed to fill the whole block, town, world: "Allah is the greatest. I bear witness that there is none worthier of worship except Allah."

These words resonated through the streets of Baghdad. The bewitching, haunting, and gentle voice caused me to slow down and sense Allah encircling me like a long noodle. Even though I didn't understand the words or believe in Islam, I welcomed the call. Years later, the call to prayer I would hear over Arabic radio or television stations, stirred in me the desire to kneel on the ground, press my palms together, and pray. It also lulled me into slumber, a dangerous matter when driving a car, operating a machine, or handling a carton of eggs.

I joined the ladies sitting on the beautiful burgundy rug with beige and light green symmetrical designs. Several of them approached me to introduce themselves and answer my questions. I learned that most of the attendees were from Bangladesh with others from surrounding South Asian countries. This masjid had been around for approximately three years, and its location was temporary as a larger one was being built a few miles further north. It was always available for prayer but on the first Friday of every month, there was a community gathering where everyone brought food and ate together, prayed, and then listened to the speaker of the month give a lecture.

I felt at home, although I had expected a different setup for the lecture, one that resembled those held at classrooms, offices, banquet halls, and libraries where people sat in rows and a few, like myself, wrote down the speaker's every word on paper. The email invitation said that Dawud Walid was going to give a lecture at the AMDA Masjid about the importance of recognizing and properly addressing extreme religious rhetoric in Islam. Dawud is Michigan's executive director of CAIR (Council on American Islamic Relations). We had met previously and given talks at some of the same conferences. He is also part of a documentary that I was working on at the time, *The Great American Family*. We once talked about possibly organizing a type of forum to open dialogue between Muslims and Christians here in Michigan. Noticing today's lecture was conveniently located minutes away from home, and liking the subject matter, I decided to go.

The lively conversations around me were no different than the usual topics women tended to cover—weddings, food, friendships, breastfeeding, motherhood, nails, etc. The younger ladies dressed exquisitely and were nicely groomed. All appeared to be university students. The food ranged from mashed eggplants to mashed dry fish, slow braised pot roast, steamed rice cakes, and other delicious dishes and desserts. The lecture was something we don't hear about in Islamic and non-Islamic media outlets alike. Dawud talked about the importance of American Muslims having good manners towards differences of opinion. "In other Muslim communities around the world, each town and village may follow one school of thought," he said. "But there's a diverse pluralistic community called America where many different ethnicities live. So we have to open our minds and be flexible to others' opinions. Just because we don't understand something does not make it wrong or un-Islamic."

He encouraged that instead, people give advice, if they're qualified to do so (he noticed the worst debaters on Islam are those who know nothing about it). And if they do give advice, to do so in the manner the Quran asks for—with tenderness and gentleness so that they do not commit verbal aggression on each other and so no one feels slighted or embarrassed.

"In Islam there are some things that are non-negotiable, but most are flexible," he said. "We shouldn't let our small differences disunite us as a community. Scholars debated centuries ago about such matters as whether the Quran is a word of God or if it is the creation of God, and about other matters. They never sorted out those questions, so we don't have to get bogged down about it." Another quote he used from the Quran was "Let there be no compulsion in religion because right action is clear from error"—meaning, he added, anytime we use pressure to make someone do something against their will, they will naturally hate it.

I left the masjid that night feeling as though I had visited South Asia for a few hours, and happy that a leader supported the idea that religion isn't about pressuring people to follow rules. The next day, I bundled my daughter and son, drove to Lifetime Fitness, and dropped them off at the daycare center where members could leave their children for up to two hours. I then walked to the athletic country club's café to meet with Lance Kawas, a producer friend and formerly my screenwriting instructor at film school. He had taken interest in my thesis, a short film called *Green Card Wedding*, and advised me to turn it into a feature film. I wrote the script and we decided to collaborate on this project.

I told Lance about my experience at the masjid and he said that people have created so many divisions when really we are all cousins who stem from Prophet Abraham, and that today, if Prophet Muhammad or Jesus saw what we were doing to each other, they would turn around and go back into their graves. "All this fighting is not about religion," he said. "It's about real estate."

He said quite a few interesting things, some of which I knew; that Jesus and all the prophets are revered in the Quran; that Mary is the only woman mentioned. In fact, Surah 19, one of the longest chapters in the Quran, is titled "Maryam" which means Mary. One of the stories that I didn't know was about the document that Prophet Muhammed wrote to St. Catherine's Monastery, the world's oldest continuously inhabited monastery, located at the foot of Mount Sinai in Egypt. The document is hung inside the monastery along with a large collection of other manuscripts, outnumbered only by the Vatican Library. The translation is as follows:

The Promise to St. Catherine:

This is a message from Muhammad ibn Abdullah, as a covenant to those who adopt Christianity, near and far, we are with them. Verily I, the servants, the helpers, and

my followers defend them, because Christians are my citizens; and by Allah! I hold out against anything that dis-
pleases them.

No compulsion is to be on them. Neither are their
judges to be removed from their jobs nor their monks from
their monasteries. No one is to destroy a house of their
religion, to damage it, or to carry anything from it to the
Muslims' houses. Should anyone take any of these, he would
spoil God's covenant and disobey His Prophet. Verily, they
are my allies and have my secure charter against all that
they hate. No one is to force them to travel or to oblige
them to fight.

The Muslims are to fight for them. If a female Christian
is married to a Muslim, it is not to take place without her
approval. She is not to be prevented from visiting her church
to pray. Their churches are to be respected. They are neither to be prevented from repairing them nor the sacredness of their covenants. No one of the nation (Muslims) is
to disobey the covenant till the Last Day (end of the world).

I was delighted to learn of this letter until I came across additional material that set my mood back to square one. Muslim
and Western Scholars have questioned the authenticity of these
covenants, multiple in number, claiming they were forged by
Christians intent on proving to their Muslim overlords that
the Prophet himself had guaranteed their well-being and the
preservation of their property. Gabriel Said Reynolds, professor of Islamic Studies and Theology at the University of Notre
Dame, writes, "The earliest copies of the 'Covenant of the
Prophet with the Monks of Mt. Sinai' date to the sixteenth century (over nine hundred years after the death of Muhammad).
The 'Covenant of the Prophet with Assyrian Christians' dates
to the seventeenth century and is in an Islamic Persian script

that did not exist in Muhammad's day, and the 'Covenant of the Prophet with the Christians of the World,' which includes twenty-two signatures meant to be those of the Prophet's companions, dates to the sixteenth."

The criticism made me wonder why humans even bother trusting dusty books or manuscripts when they are written and rewritten over and over again. I had wondered this as I witnessed after the 2003 US-led invasion of Iraq, the killings, kidnappings and bombings targeted against Christians. There were many incidences of Christians being brutally killed for wearing a cross or clergy attires. Church bombings spread across the country, the worst one occurring on October 31, 2010 when Islamic militants seized Our Lady of Salvation Catholic Church in Baghdad during Sunday evening mass, killing dozens of people. I ended up covering protests of black-clad demonstrators in Metro Detroit demanding peace for Christians.

I wondered the same thing as I witnessed, two years after I was introduced to the disputed covenant, ISIS capture Mosul in northern Iraq. They seized the buildings of the Chaldean Catholic Archdiocese and the Assyrian Orthodox Diocese and began placing marks on minorities' properties to designate them as Christians, Shabak, or Shia Turkmen. Aside from painting homes with the letter "N" for *Nasrani*, they wrote the phrase "Properties of the Islamic State." They levied a "jihad tax" on minorities and began killing and kidnapping them, including nuns and orphans. Tens of thousands of families fled. Within a few months, the oldest towns of Nineveh Plains were practically emptied of its indigenous people.

I ended up covering anti-ISIS protests in Metro Detroit because of these atrocities. During the same time, I also covered an event to commemorate the Simile Massacre in 1933 when the Iraqi Army began their assault on hundreds of villages near Dohuk and Mosul, causing the death of thousands of Christian men, women, and children. Most of the survivors fled to neighboring countries.

I did the reporting with a calm composure and professional standpoint, but inside I felt pain and grief. After I submitted the articles to my editor, I wanted to scatter this horrific subject outside like breadcrumbs, let the birds carry it away, and forget about it forever.

A pleasant distraction appeared before my eyes shortly thereafter, like the genie in Aladdin, and drew me into a magical situation. My husband and I planned a trip to Vegas for our ten-year anniversary. I'm not the Vegas type, he is, but I was ready to visit a land known for its utmost freedom and exciting night life. I agreed to go as long as I could pick the hotel. The Venetian Resort seemed to have precious Italian treasures that would nurture my heart as a writer and explorer. Once again, I could be the tourist of my younger years, lost in the cobbled streets of Europe. It was the first time since our honeymoon that we'd gone on a trip alone.

We barely situated ourselves when, one early morning, I received a text from the editor of *The Chaldean News* asking if I could cover the story of the town hall meeting. *What town hall meeting?* Sterling Heights City Council was to vote on the construction of a proposed mega mosque (20,500 square foot to be exact) that had for years been met with controversial opposition from the community, prompting federal intervention. Sterling Heights already had two mosques, and within less than a year of ISIS destroying the villages in northern Iraq, local Shia Muslims wanted to build a third one in a residential neighborhood where many Christian refugees, who fled Islamic persecution in Iraq, were living.

The American Islamic Community Center's application for a permit was rejected after the city determined that its proposed use was incompatible with the residential area. Too much traffic and too little parking, so the city planning commission decided by a 9-0 vote against the mosque in September 2015. Hundreds of Sterling Heights residents gathered outside City Hall to celebrate. That celebration was caught on video, and critics cited it as evidence that the city was biased against Muslims.

In December, the mosque sued the city, so the Obama Justice Department stepped in and claimed that the real reason the mosque was denied was because the city was catering to anti-Muslim bigotry in the community. Residents feared it was a bad deal, like the one where the Obama DOJ forced nearby Pittsfield Township to pay out $1.7 million to local Muslims, in repudiation for denying a permit for an Islamic School. Township employees were also ordered to undergo sensitivity training to ensure they never again discriminate against Muslims. All this happened just one year prior.

I told my editor that I was out of town, and as I got out of bed, I considered this peculiar coincidence. In the eight years I'd worked for *The Chaldean News* I had not once turned down a major story. Living on the "East Side," I was the go-to reporter for events on my side of town. My knowledge of three languages—Arabic, Aramaic, and English—came in handy when we had delegates that traveled here from Iraq or other Arabic countries. And now, my unavailability was a godsend. I loved being as neutral as Switzerland. I suppose I was destined to be so. After all, I was given the name Weam, which translates to peace and harmony.

While my husband slept, I got dressed as quietly as possible, took my journal and pen, and stepped out of our room. I strolled over the gleaming marble floors of the Venetian, framed with Italian inspired classical art and architecture, and I strolled under the hand-painted fresco that adorned the ceilings, all hand-painted by Italian artists. Although they weren't

Michelangelo's paintings, I delighted in gazing over their gorgeous touch.

I arrived at St. Mark's Square, a smaller scaled model of the historical square in Venice, minus the Adriatic Sea and the estimated hundred thousand pigeons and sixty thousand residents living there. Here, Vegas entertainers and singers occasionally walked about the square full of shops and restaurants. The water and bridges dominated the center of the shops, and the gondolas floated through the canals. The atmosphere took me back to my month-long visit to Rome and the short trips south, to Sicily of course, because that's where *The Godfather* was filmed. I did not visit Venice but learned that when Napoleon and his army descended on that city in 1797, the French general described this immense open public space that's almost forty thousand square feet as "the drawing room of Europe."

I entered a restaurant, ordered coffee and a croissant, and carried them to the upper-level floor. I sat on a table overlooking the St. Mark's Square replica and began to journal. I did not know how to feel about the mosque controversy. It was a hot topic with a lot of ingredients and flavors that boiled to the rim of the pot, partially spilling over to the cooler areas, creating a mess on the stove and a fear that someone would get burned by the fire. Separatism is a common practice in the Middle East where ethnic cleansing and genocide are repeated themes. In the United States, people *try* to put a lid on separatism. They attempt, though not always successfully, to cook the soup and serve it as a delicious meal for everyone to share. Once the soup's vegetables and seasoning are mixed and slowly simmered, there's no separating the broccoli florets from the cauliflower florets without one having influenced the other.

In the afternoon, my husband and I went for a long walk on the busy strip. I happily passed out money to veterans and paraplegics in wheelchairs. He made sure he carried small bills in his wallet so I could. We visited different hotels that represented different countries, cities, or regions such as Egypt, Paris, New York, the Roman Empire, and Polynesia. In the evening, we watched opera singers perform songs mixed with drama and comedy that reverberated off the walls. When we hit the street at night, we noticed an immense number of hookers everywhere and homeless men and women lying on the floor with cardboard signs asking for money to buy weed.

"At least they're honest," my husband said, matter-of-factly.

My husband and I were both born in Iraq but had a different upbringing, since I left my birth country for America before the Iraq-Iran War had begun in late1980. I did not witness any war. He was barely ten years old when the Iraq-Iran war happened. He experienced the forty-two days of relentless consecutive bombing of Iraq during the 1991 Gulf War, the twelve-plus years of sanctions the United Nations placed on the country, and a lot more struggles and hardships before he made it to the United States.

I lost contact with my friends back home while he stayed in contact with them, especially his college friends. Eleven guys formed a friendship at Al Rafidain University College the year they started in 1991 and maintained it long after graduating in 1997. Five left Iraq to live elsewhere, including my husband. One guy began a messenger group called "The naughties of Al Rafidain University" and brought them back together—except for one friend they could not find. The group is majority Muslim, with one Mandean and one Christian, my husband.

To this day, these friends call each other on holidays. I often overhear them managing conflict with humor. "Hey brother, you're still alive? *Daesh* (ISIS) didn't get a hold of you yet? A bomb didn't go off in your house?" followed by a lot of obscenities and laughter. My husband tells me stories of his college days; which girl liked which guy, which guy liked which girl, and the innocence that existed between the sexes back then. Men respected their female classmates and never took advantage of them, whereas nowadays, things are different, his friends tell him. Boys and girls go to a *sheikh* and pay a small fee for a marriage license so they can rent a hotel room (in Iraq couples can't rent a room without showing proof of marriage). Afterward, the two get divorced.

One of my favorite stories of his is when one of his friends took him to Sheikh Saad, located in a countryside southeast of Baghdad. He entered his home, made of sun-dried brick and clay, and was told to stay put in a certain spot. "My aunts keep after me to show them what a Christian looks like," his friend said, but his sentences were sprinkled with profanities. Some women then drew open the curtains and peeked through, their *abaya* covering most of their face. Only their eyes shown. "My goodness, he looks like us! He has a nose and mouth like we do! The Prophet's light is upon him!"

My husband cussed out his friend and asked, "What, am I a monkey at the zoo?"

The men had a good laugh afterward.

I returned from Vegas to witness the Sterling Heights community in a verbal confrontation with each other. Across the street from the proposed mosque, signs made it clear that the mosque was not welcome: "We don't want it!" "Sensitivity works both ways… if you really care, build it elsewhere!" American flags flapped in the summer breeze. *The Detroit Free Press* reported that "The dispute sparked tensions between some Middle Eastern Christians and Muslims in Metro Detroit, leading to a war of words on social media. Problems in the Middle East added to the tensions, and both sides accusingly compared each other to ISIS extremists."

To diffuse the tensions, the head of the Chaldean Church in Metro Detroit, Bishop Francis Kalabat met with Imam Hassan al-Qazwini at the Iraqi Consulate office in Southfield. Both of Iraqi descent, they wanted to encourage dialogue over the issue. And Steve Spreitzer, president and CEO of the Michigan Roundtable for Diversity and Inclusion, called for greater understanding of Islam, noting the prejudices that some Catholics and Jews faced in the nineteenth and twentieth centuries when they tried to open their centers in the United States.

In Dearborn, some Arab-American Muslims slammed the attacks on the mosque. Tarek Baydoun, a Muslim attorney, sent an automated voicemail to eighteen thousand homes in Sterling Heights that said in part: "Perhaps the greatest difference between the United States and Iraq is that in the United States, our government does not take sides between religions. Some people that came here in search of religious liberty and personal freedom want the city government to enforce their opinions on others. This is simply unacceptable, and fundamentally un-American."

The boxing match continued, and I watched. A number of sentiments spewing from my Chaldean community were distasteful, some straight out horrible, and quite frankly, embarrassing. Several non-Chaldeans gushed hatred as well, one man pointing out that he'd served in Iraq during the war and that he'd seen what "those people were like." My desire to call for cooperation and reconciliation between people, any people, wanted me to shake them up and say, "Stop it! Behave like adults." But I didn't shake them, and they didn't stop.

When Trump ran for presidency in 2016, the Chaldean community banded together to vote him in. That was their retaliation, some suppose. But they also believed he would be a good president for the economy and the Christians. He would protect them, they thought, and help them gain security and rights in the Nineveh Plains in Iraq, the areas that were taken over by ISIS.

Then one hot summer Sunday in June of 2017, I found myself once again covering a protest in Sterling Heights that had to do with Iraqi Christians. U.S. Immigration and Customs Enforcement (ICE) detained over a hundred Iraqi-born people, rounding them up from their homes, churches, restaurants, and one elderly was even taken out of the hospital. The detained had not entered the United States illegally but most had lost their green card status for having at some point broken the law. Most of their cases were low-level, nonviolent crimes committed decades ago, often a marijuana possession charge that was once a felony and today is a misdemeanor. Most had long since paid their debt to society and kept a clean record, worked, and paid taxes.

The detainees were taken to the ICE field offices in Detroit and placed on three buses. Friends and family watched from behind a barred fence, weeping and screaming in agony. One woman repeatedly shouted, "Trump tricked us!" A woman, overcome with fear for her husband, fainted. Another came away with bruises on her arm from the police restraining her because she refused to let her brother go "just like this." Several people jumped in front of the moving vehicles. Being deported to Iraq then, when ISIS still controlled much of the country, especially with the tattoo of the Christian cross on your wrist, which many Chaldeans had, was a death sentence.

While my family had not been directly affected, a number of our friends and our children's schoolmates were. In my children's elementary school, students who had a loved one detained didn't show up to class for days, or weeks. During my walks in my neighborhood, I saw tall red crosses planted in people's yards, indicating a loved one was detained, and signs that read "Stop the Deportation."

In response, Iraqi leaders, activists, and organizations quickly went to work to fight the mass deportations of Iraqi nationals, mostly Christians. As early as Monday, June 12 at two in the morning, Nathan Kalasho, then the director of KEYS Grace Academy Charter School, posted on his Facebook Page "To my community… we need to galvanize. This will not be tolerated. We will not allow our members to be victims of this inhumane treatment." An hour later, he posted a community call to action, asking immigration attorneys, volunteers, and families of those that have been detained to come to KEYS Grace Academy at 9:45 p.m. This initiated an around-the-clock effort led by CODE Legal Aid, a non-profit organization that's dedicated to providing legal advocacy and assistance to those in need. The next day, Martin Manna, president and CEO of the Chaldean Community Foundation, hosted a meeting with retired Senator Carl Levin, the John Ashcroft Law Firm, American Civil Liberties Union (ACLU), International Refugee Assistance Project (IRAP), CODE Legal Aid, KEYS Grace Academy and several immigration attorneys and community leaders to discuss efforts to stop deportations. Within less than two weeks, a federal judge in Detroit halted the deportation of more than 1,400 Iraqis (Christian and Muslim) nationwide, allowing the Iraqis to challenge their deportation on a case-to-case basis in federal court.

Some people confided in me that, "Well, what goes around comes around" and asked, sarcastically, "Do the Chaldeans still support Trump?" Other similar comments were thrown like snowballs between the Democrats and Republicans. Two years later, I covered the story of Jimmy Al-Daoud who died on the streets of Baghdad after being deported to Iraq.

The whole heartbreaking situation disturbed and exhausted me.

Once upon a time, the Muslim call to prayer that resonated through Baghdad's streets held a lovely memory for me. The mesmerizing, soothing verses, sung in a poetic and harmonious tone, disconnected me from the material world and brought me closer to the Creator. It caused me to stop in my tracks to listen to the essence of my soul. That is what adhan means; to listen.

Over time, this feeling of innocence was washed away by teaspoonfuls of bitter flavors regularly touching my palate. I tried to spit out the bitterness that tasted like cold and molded leftover tealeaves. I wanted to wipe it from memory, but other negative incidences kept occurring. The idea of making a fresh pot of *chai* sounded invigorating right around the time of Trump's new presidency, a time which widened the tensions between the Christians and Muslims. Perhaps I could introduce a new recipe, though it might be true that there's nothing new under the sun.

Chai means tea. The word originated in China. The British brought the tea plants to India from China, as they had taken a liking to the drink. It traveled to other parts of the world as well, and today, Arabs, Turks, Indonesians, Swahilis, Slavs (except for the Polish), use chai to describe tea. Indian chai is my favorite, with its distinct spices and warm and soothing flavors that often include milk and sugar. I too could combine a variety of ingredients such as mint, love, peace, harmony, humor, freedom, and honey, and like hot delicious tea, serve it as a story for family, friends, and even strangers to enjoy. The idea thrilled me, giving me the energy and inspiration necessary for the task.

So I sat down and wrote a movie script that later turned into a book. It was about an Iraqi Muslim family and their

Iraqi Christian neighbors living in the US, more specifically, in "Little Baghdad." There was so much buzz around the story that I was invited to talk about it on a platform that was all about celebrating interfaith diversity. *The Detroit News* featured an article about it in their entertainment section with the headline "Local Iraqi-American film, novel aims to bring unity between Chaldean, Muslim communities." I never imagined that such attempts at a contemporary interfaith story would lead to my first book talk cancellation in seventeen years.

Chapter 6

THE MAKING OF *POMEGRANATE*

"I'm sorry to inform you that we've decided to cancel the *Pomegranate* talk because of all the tension that was created in the Muslim community due to the story line in the book about the Muslim woman wanting to remove her hijab… There was a lot of heated discussion about this… Your book has created such controversy in the Muslim faith… I'm looking forward to seeing the *Pomegranate* movie and I have enjoyed reading your book!!"

My eyes riveted to the top of the email, and I reread each word, chewing it carefully as if it were a piece of unchewable steak. The double exclamation points did not create the positive tone the sender obviously hoped for. Instead, it tasted like a rotten garnish over the inedible meal, and it gave me heartburn.

I sighed. My first talk cancelation in my entire career! The Jewish woman who sent the email was the same person who invited me to speak at her interfaith group. An interfaith book cancelled by an interfaith group! I recalled a quote emphasizing the importance of dialogue among Abrahamic religions, "We human beings today face a stark choice: dialogue or death!" Whether one considered cancel culture a godsend or a modern-day Frankenstein, it was undoubtedly growing fatter than a massive blue whale, which can measure up to a hundred feet long and weigh over two hundred tons. According to the BBC, this animal has the biggest percentage of body fat on land and sea.

"Dear so-and-so," I typed in response, followed by a long-winded speech about how this sad situation resembled the way in which people in the Middle East reject, and even kill, different viewpoints, especially when it concerns women. "You'd think that living in the United States people would learn to embrace true diversity, not only their one-sided version of it," I typed with furious restraint, adding that this was, nevertheless, not surprising. "As part of this community, I have observed for decades how it continues to struggle here in the United States and especially in the Middle East. The community seems unable, or unwilling, to understand how important freedom of expression is—along with a general refusal to engage in healthy and honest dialogue."

I pressed send, and my attention went from my laptop to the television. I was sitting on the couch in the living room. The kids were in their bedrooms, my husband at work. The news anchor went on and on about how Biden should resign after a sexual harassment report. I lowered the volume and thought of the many other things I wanted to ask and say as I reread the email. Who were the Muslims you were referring to? No Muslims in my circle support those kinds of ideologies which have destroyed relationships between the Jewish, Christian, and Muslim communities in the Middle East. And they definitely don't want them to sneak into the American way of life. Most of the Muslim women I knew never wore a hijab, had removed it long ago, or wore it by choice and enjoyed a fairly modern and privileged lifestyle. The general community agreed (at least in public) that it was not mandatory to wear the hijab.

I stopped arguing in my head, told my thoughts to go away, got up from the couch, and sauntered into the kitchen to make a cup of coffee. It was a hot August afternoon. The entire week had been layered with eighty-degree temperatures and lots of cinematic drama. I'd stayed up until the wee hours the night before talking on the phone with Scott Rosenfelt, the executive producer of *Pomegranate.* He was working on a film in the Philippines, which is thirteen hours ahead of Michigan, but we had a dilemma to resolve. The girl who was to play "Mary" in our film signed on with another project without notifying us. We were scheduled to start filming in a little over a month.

"Welcome to Hollywood!" Scott said, with a slight laugh that I enjoyed hearing. It put me at ease because it had the "not surprised" "been there, done that" and "no big deal" attitude. Having him as part of this project somehow made me feel safe and secure. Scott had tried to negotiate a deal with the actress's manager and agent, to rearrange our schedule to meet her availability. That meant we'd either shoot the film in the winter or in the spring of the following year. "Spring is three seasons away," I said, "and winters in Michigan are cold and snowy. It won't align with the time-period of the film, and it would hinder a lot of creative control."

"I understand," he said, "but cross your fingers and pray." Then he told me a story. When they started making *Smoke Signals* on an Indian reservation, the weather was crappy. They had a shaman come out on the morning of their first day. The shaman blessed the film and it all worked out. "Have faith," he said. "Weather should not be your worry."

Yes, that's the answer—praying and having faith. My mind and body suddenly relaxed and surrendered to the process. For the first time since he and I met, I told him that I had studied shamanism for four years with bestselling author and mystic Lynn V. Andrews. She was married to Kurt Neumann Jr., the former head of feature films at Warner Brothers Studios. I met her in 2011, and in recent years, I mentored her apprentices. Lynn, the ancient teachings, and her mentors helped me heal a great deal of trauma that was the result of being born in an oppressive region. Their wisdom, blessings, and belief in me were life changing.

He was amazed by this information, said he knew who Lynn was. What was even more amazing was that Kurt was the executive at Warner Brothers when Scott was there making *Home Alone*. He spoke to him every day. The movie moved to another studio, 20th Century Fox, because of an escalating budget, the news reported, though Scott said that some of the Warner Brothers executives didn't understand how a couple of young producers and a young director could make a good movie. The film went on to gross nearly $286 million. "Warner Brothers kicked themselves for years about that decision!" he said, laughing.

"You know, you can look in your community for a 'Mary,'" Scott said. "You might discover a talent who will make her acting debut in *Pomegranate*."

I reflected on that advice. The next evening, as my family hurried to get ready for a wedding, my daughter, disappointed with how one cousin did her hair, called another cousin to come and save the day. She said, "Mom, Natally is coming to do my hair."

"What?!" I said, half-dressed, and my brain spinning. "We don't have time!"

"She's down the street, at McDonald's," she explained, her face flushed and her eyes avoiding mine. "She has all the hair products in her car."

"Your hair looks beautiful as it is, why make a fuss? And you were supposed to straighten my hair, remember?!"

Amid my complaints, the front door opened wide, and our cousin Natally walked in. She properly said her hellos and casually strolled into my daughter's bedroom. They unearthed a solution for getting both our hair done simultaneously. We situated ourselves in a row; I sat on the vanity stool facing the mirror, my daughter stood behind me doing my hair and Natally stood behind her doing her hair. As they chatted with each other, I observed Natally through the mirror. She was a petite 20-year-old woman with long curly hair, brown eyes, and a confident attitude.

"Natally, have you ever done acting?" I asked, remembering Scott's words.

"Yes, I have," she said, her eyes widening. "When I was in high school…"

As my daughter straightened my hair strands, and Natally straightened my daughter's hair strands, I listened to Natally's passion for theatre, singing, and video production. She had created short films that showcased her talent, and she participated in on-stage musical productions of *Greece*, *Thoroughly Modern Millie*, and more. She also participated in the Michigan Solo Ensemble Festival three years in a row where she received a superior medal her last two years. In college, she produced, wrote, and directed a short film showcasing the stigma surrounding mental illness.

"Do you want to audition for my film?" I asked the now grown woman that was once the flower girl at my wedding.

"Yes, I'd love to!"

Natally got the part for "Mary." We were lucky that the first actress bailed out because I found the talent I didn't know I was looking for. A first-generation Chaldean American, Natally represented the character she was playing. This was the case with our lead "Niran," the Iraqi Muslim immigrant, and most of our cast. It was serendipity at its finest.

I poured a tablespoon of Nescafe into the boiling cup of water. Its aroma, and its seamless dancing steam that resembled an exotic belly dancer, along with the sun beaming through the window put me in a state of euphoria. In my quiet home, I took a sip of the delicious coffee, then closed my eyes to rise above the trees and into the clouds so I could focus on the present. *Pomegranate* was set to become the first Iraqi American feature film, with a writer, director, and cast made up of the community it represents. The story highlights the beauty, harmony, and realistic struggles and conflicts of Arabs and Chaldeans in America.

It had a peculiar journey, this story, starting off as a script, which Francis Coppola's *Zoetrope* selected as quarter finalist. It caught the interest of story consultant Dr. Stan Williams, who was my former instructor at film school and author of *The Moral Premise: Harnessing Virtue and Vice for Box Office Success*, which Will Smith considered, "The most powerful tool in my new tool box." Stan helped me revise the script and offered guidance during the development stage. Later, Buffalo 8, a production company in Santa Monica, California, got involved with pre-production. During casting, I consulted with my inner guide, which you can call my Fairy Godmother, to transform the story into another format. Without hesitation, she lifted her wand and turned *Pomegranate* into a novel. The pumpkin, I mean novel, carried me closer to each character and deeper into developing their lives and the world they inhabit, preparing me to direct my first feature narrative.

I had directed my first feature documentary by this time, which won two international awards. But documentaries capture reality, and the script is often written after filming has begun. *Pomegranate* was a pre-scripted movie with actors. Stan recommended I read a popular book on directing actors. I felt that I had already studied directing at this point. For twelve years, I managed our family-owned video store where I watched and rewatched remarkable films during my shifts. Then, I went to film school for one year. Nonetheless, I bought the book to get more pointers and valuable insights. What I got instead were loads of conflicting advice teeter-tottering on the same pages: Remember this, don't forget that, but the opposite may apply. It was bewildering and counterintuitive, so I decided to close the book and rely on the experience and education I already had; the human-awareness I'd developed as a writer, poet, journalist, filmmaker, and spiritual seeker; the decades I'd spent talking with and listening to people from all walks of life; my bachelor's degree in communication.

The magic dust that sprinkled out of *Pomegranate* led to Scott becoming our executive producer. He loved the story's originality, humor, and importance. *Pomegranate* is about Niran, a Muslim woman coming of age in Sterling Heights after emigrating from Iraq. She's bold and politically liberal in the face of her family's strict culture. On top of that, she lives in a predominantly conservative Chaldean neighborhood. Niran is inspired to follow her dreams by her idol, Enheduanna, the first recorded writer in history and a famed princess and priestess of Ancient Mesopotamia. Our cast, led by women talent, were grateful and excited to play roles of relatable characters that are colorful rather than pretentious, negative, dehumanizing, and saturated with lyrical self-indulgence. I was proud of what I'd accomplished. Then this…

I opened my eyes and sighed in exasperation. A sense of confusion and disappointment consumed me. I live in a free-thinking society where you are constantly, I mean constantly, told that you can craft your legacy, however you wish, even if it's challenging, even if you live under unbearable circumstances, even amongst those who discourage you and try to hold you back. While to some people this might sound like wishful thinking, an imaginary thing, a ploy to get money from the most gullible people, this mindset has created more peaceful, creative, successful, and interesting societies in comparison to the mindset of preordained destiny. It has helped me make amazing things happen.

When the sun set and the temperature dropped, I took my dog Teddy on our daily walk in the shady streets that were filled with an abundance of green lawns, trees, flowers, plants, and wildlife. The variety of birds and small mammals brought to surface that instinctual nature that most human beings repress in civilized life. In this area, I've seen foxes and coyotes run by, raccoons and opossum come to my door, and once, my friend and I heard a lion roar.

Smelling the flowering trees from a distance, I reflected on what had occurred earlier in the day. I felt dis-courage-d that once again my community failed to en-courage me. They let me down so many times that I often wanted to stop trying. Everything I've worked toward had taken a lot longer than expected since I worked, took care of the children, did the house chores, cooked, cleaned, washed laundry, and ran errands. I was even my mother's caregiver for five years. I had to work harder and smarter so I would not fall into an inspirational regression.

My thoughts were interrupted by the sight of the two old women who were related to my husband, a widow and her sister-in-law, sitting on the front porch. One was in her mid-eighties and the other in her mid-nineties. They had lived together ever since the widow married the maiden's brother. When we first moved to this neighborhood, we often saw them driving and walking side-by-side up-and-down the street. Now that they were aging, they no longer did that. The widow told me in Aramaic, "We're expired," meaning they were done, finished, caput, adding that her children took away her license and sold her classic black Mercedes because they did not want her to drive anymore.

"They're worried for your safety," I said.

"No, they said, 'Mom, we don't want you killing anyone on the street.'"

I tried not to smile and assured her that they must be worried about her as well.

"Me?" she said, looking at her small fragile body. My eyes followed and I noticed how thin she'd become. I could see her ribcage. "I'm already expired," she said and turned toward her sister-in-law who remained seated. "So is she. We are both expired."

I held back from bursting into laughter. She blessed me and my family as she returned to her seat next to her sister-in-law. I continued to walk, thankful for the interruption that distracted me from muddling over this book cancelation and hijab controversy. Teddy wobbled happily, having waited later than usual for our routine walk. The shih tzu, like all dogs with short flat noses, has difficulty breathing and may overheat in hot weather, so we must exercise earlier or later in the day when the weather is cooler.

From a distance I saw my younger brother walking his dog, Prince. I called out to him, and as usual our dogs froze to assess the situation and then sprinted toward each other. My brother and I met halfway and continued our walk together. We passed under a large wisteria tree and a few lavender-colored petals fell on us. We stopped to greet some of the four-legged friends of our dogs, allowing the pets to play and sniff each other, and pulling them away when they tried to claim social territory via urination.

I shared with my brother what had happened. He was surprised but shrugged it off. That's how we are. When you're a minority of a minority of a minority, like Christian Iraqis are, you learn to keep your head down and show, not tell, the world who you are, as you silently deal with the feelings provoked in you: the feelings of helplessness, hopelessness, shame, and loss of self-worth. You understand that other groups have suffered equal or worse colonialism, like the Indians, Native Americans, Mexicans, and some Africans. You find ways to navigate your negative emotions through your family, community, faith, and by overcompensating for your losses and humiliations.

My brother and I agreed that silencing freedom of speech and preventing opportunities for a healthy debate in the United States was tyrannical, and it led to violence and war. It was the very thing our family escaped from in Iraq, where my father was punished for criticizing the Baath Party.

"You know what bothers me?" I asked him. He didn't say a word, signaling for me to go on. We stepped to the side, giving room for upcoming bikers. "A scholar and author by the name Dr. Jack Shaheen wrote a book called *Reel Bad Arabs*. It's over six hundred pages of study on how Hollywood vilifies Muslims and Arabs."

While people passed us by—mothers with baby strollers, pet owners with their dogs, kids on scooters and roller skates—I told him about the day I met Dr. Shaheen. We sat next to each other at a conference where we both gave a talk. I shared with him that I'm a filmmaker, working on a documentary about an American woman of Iraqi descent who received an unjust trial. As a result, she was currently serving time in federal prison. His face slightly contorted. His smile remained but became inflicted with awkwardness. I was silent for the rest of our encounter, and so was he.

Shaheen's study was basically a reference book with an alphabetical list of films, each with a short summary of how Arabs are portrayed in Hollywood. Not one page contains a discussion on the content of any of the films, or the history of the film industry, particularly as it pertains to the Middle East.

Film was an invention of the West that began in the late

nineteenth century. At the time, European countries had occupied much of the Middle East. These countries introduced film to the Arab world. In those early days, cinema flourished in Northern Africa, especially in Egypt, where films by the Lumiere brothers were first screened in 1896. Slowly and waveringly, the medium began to spread throughout the Arab world. The period between the 1940s and 1960s was considered the golden age of Egyptian cinema.

In Saudi Arabia, cinema was not accepted, however, until the 60s and 70s. Then in the early 1980s it was banned for thirty-five years. Yemen has kept its movie theaters closed since the end of the twentieth century, and music and public entertainment is only admitted on TV shows or for special occasions, such as weddings. Over the decades, Egyptian cinema experienced a downward spiral as it became more of a slave to politics and religion. And in recent years, Arab women who use media or films as a freedom of expression are experiencing more and more backlash, risk imprisonment and even death. In Iraq, prominent women that ranged from lawyers to social media influencers were shot and killed, and since no serious investigations into their murders took place, many began to suspect a coordinated campaign to silence outspoken women.

"Dr. Shaheen gave no solutions in his book," I said, "no self-examination of how maybe, our own communities, who are capable to support filmmakers if they choose, are contributing to this lack of presence in Hollywood."

When the first Netflix Original Arabic Series was released in 2019, called *Jinn*, Jordan's top prosecutor demanded the cybercrimes department to halt the broadcast. He launched an investigation and tried to summon individuals and entities involved in the production of the series. The cast and crew suffered bullying, even though they made the film "to show off what we have in the Arab World." In 2022, conservative leaders in Egypt called to ban *Perfect Strangers* due to homosexuality, sexual infidelity, and sex positivity. Had I lived in those countries, I too could be banned, or worse. Again and again, efforts to provide a broader perspective on Arab culture through film and media are stopped, not encouraged. Sad to say, the Middle East is contributing to a narrow representation of itself.

The "Entertainment Media Use in the Middle East" 2014 survey, commissioned by Northwestern University and the Doha Film Institute, interviewed more than six thousand people—both nationals and expats—in Qatar, Saudi Arabia, Lebanon, Egypt, Tunisia, and the United Arab Emirates. According to the survey, 45 percent of respondents said they watch Hollywood movies, but 34 percent said American films have content that is "harmful to morality." Respondents in Saudi Arabia and Egypt show the strongest support for censorship—76 percent and 77 percent respectively.

Two months after the release of Dr. Shaheen's book, 9/11 happened. And the image of terrorists in Hollywood was now on our local news channels for days and years to come.

Eventually my brother and I went our separate ways and headed home. The day was nearly done and the experiences nearly over. I let go of the book cancelation because I didn't want to carry it with me to sleep. I preferred to remember the bookstore I discovered at the Venetian in Vegas. It was called Bauman's Rare Books. Walking through it felt as if walking through a literary museum. There were first editions and classics that cost as much as a house, and a sign that invited guests to "Ask us to show you how to handle unique books"—a polite and dignified way to state that the visit would be a "look don't touch" experience. The bookstore *touched me* like *Gone with the Wind* and other Western literature that continued to influence my imagination. Arab literature, on the other hand, was bogged down by politics and religion and rarely were women the heroine of the story.

I did love *Guests of the Sheik: An Ethnography of an Iraqi Village* written by Elizabeth Warnock Fernea, an author, scholar, filmmaker, and professor of comparative literature and Middle East studies at the University of Texas. Elizabeth wrote a delightfully charming book about her experience living with her husband Robert, as newlyweds, in a small town in southern Iraq. Robert was conducting an anthropological study of tribal life. Elizabeth became integrated into the town and it became her home for two years, from 1957 to 1959. This was long before the nearly half-dozen wars and sanctions, so there was an opportunity to delve into the friendship of the women who at first glance seemed worlds apart. I was so moved by this book, I wrote a letter to Fernea expressing my feelings. She kindly responded.

At this point, the book cancelation was the least of my problems. Production of *Pomegranate* the movie was weighing heavy on me. My body was weak and my mind foggy. Four months prior, I had been hospitalized for five days with COVID-19. When I left the hospital, I could barely stand or breathe comfortably. Yet while working full-time, I carried the tasks of multiple departments, since budget cuts were frequent and necessary to make this film happen. I learned as I went along, took many naps throughout the day to catch my breath, and had three main people to turn to for advice on the in-and-out logistics of making a film: Sam Sako, Kevin Hewitt, and Kathryn McDermott.

Sam was our Hollywood casting director and producer. He's Chaldean American and a veteran in the film industry. Interestingly, I'd met Sam in early 2007 when I was casting actors for my first feature film which never transpired. I'd traveled to Los Angeles with my husband, our eleven-month-old baby girl, my brother, and my three adult nephews. Sam and I stayed in touch afterward, and the way in which he treated me and respected my work, it felt like he was a big brother. The experience, it seems, planted the seeds for *Pomegranate* fourteen years later. Same with Kevin, our director of photography, who I met in 2006 and planned to hire for the same feature film that never transpired. When we reconnected for *Pomegranate*, we knew this time it was for real. Kathryn worked at the Motion Picture Institute of Michigan, the school I graduated from, and made me feel welcome to reach out with any questions.

I'm grateful for Sam, Kevin, and Kathryn's support, the way they prodded me on and gave me heart when I felt like giving up as I examined the confusing insurance options, wrote up agreements for the cast and crew, filled out complicated paperwork that included signing up with a payroll company, filed for a permit from the city, figured out wardrobe, prepared the shooting schedule, searched and booked airline tickets and hotels, and went hijab shopping. With the help of my sisters and cousin, I organized the food menu and gathered items for the film set, which happened to be my house and my brother's house across the street. I had to convince our L.A. producer that, no, on our side of town, actors didn't get fancy costly trailers on independent sets. Neither our budget, nor our city's ordinance, allowed it. I worried about the COVID-19 restrictions, and if any of our cast or crew members got the virus, we'd have to halt production. I also worried about how everyone was going to get paid.

I told no one involved in the film about the cancelation except for Scott. He laughed, as he often did, but this time his laughter was deeper than before. His reaction helped me lighten up. *All was well.* I had angels, my ancestors, parents, mentors, and all those who loved and cared about me, who believed in me and in this story, backing me up, giving me courage. True I was the lone wolf in some areas, but in other areas, I had the collective intellectual, emotional, and spiritual support that could move mountains.

Eleven days after the *Pomegranate* book talk was cancelled, Afghanistan's capital city Kabul fell and was captured by the Taliban. The Taliban eventually shut down middle and high schools for girls, imposed head-to-toe coverings for women and banned female students from entering a university in Kabul because they wore colored scarves. Meanwhile, we started filming *Pomegranate*.

The first week was rocky. The day I picked up the cast and producer from the airport on September 11, we learned that the hotel had cancelled our reservation because we hadn't shown up by 6 p.m. Of course, they'd failed to share this policy with me beforehand. The out-of-towners ended up spending that night in my home and going to the hotel the next morning. Two days later, they told me that their hotel, although located in a good neighborhood, was not safe; in the middle of the night, someone broke into someone's room and cops showed up to break up a fight. I quickly changed their hotel to a nicer and more comfortable one.

A load of other complications arose. I had no idea how to fill out the countless SAG Ultra papers, we didn't have a script supervisor, and we needed to hire a camera assistant. I lost five pounds within a week and had little or no sleep. My house was so hectic that even Teddy refused to return home the first night and slept at the neighbors. He did hang out with us the rest of the time, though, and once we said, "Quiet on the set!" and the camera rolled, he didn't make a peep. Teddy had a few scenes in the movie, but he didn't always fully cooperate. He was overwhelmed by the commotion and the large number of strangers. The producer and cinematographer tried to cut him out, but I put my foot down and Teddy was on his way to stardom!

We stayed on schedule, completing a thirteen-day shoot in fourteen days. Everyone gave it their all, working together like a true family; white, black, Jewish, Muslim, and Christian men and women whose ages ranged from nine to over seventy-years-old lifted each other up for the sake of creating something beautiful and meaningful. We laughed, cried, shared personal stories, and played pranks on each other. Once, Sam snuck in my husband's picture with the rest of the photographs that "Hassina" was showing to her daughter "Niran," photos of possible suitors. Sam also did the dishes when they piled up in the sink and mopped the kitchen floor when necessary. Zain, who played "Hassina," offered to vacuum the rug in the garage when she saw me doing it, so I could do other things. My sister-in-law Zina, who catered the food and whose home was used as Mary's house, ended up driving the cast back and forth to their hotel and to other areas they needed to go. Natally, who played "Mary," saved the day when she agreed at the last minute to drive ninety-minutes one-way to pick up lighting equipment before the place closed. Lindy Lenk, our costume designer and makeup artist, juggled quite a few other jobs.

We celebrated three birthdays: on the first day of filming, Jamal Adams, our first assistant director who also became our first assistant cameraperson and later our editor; somewhere in the middle of the schedule, Sam Sako; on the last day of film, Zina. We also celebrated the day Ismail Taher, who played "Ali," reached three million followers on TikTok.

"We're making a million-dollar movie on a low-budget set," said Jamal as he and I watched the dailies, the raw, unedited footage shot during the making of the film.

I was grateful for their talents and helping hands, going above and beyond to help me and each other, and they appreciated my ability to recognize how awesome they were and to nurture their creative selves. I treated every one of them with love, patience, and respect, and drew forth the best of their abilities. Together, we had our own interfaith circle. We each stood strong in our own faith while supporting and encouraging others who dared to express themselves. We choreographed a dance that exercised muscles of love we didn't know we had. All of it happened right here in "Little Baghdad."

Shortly after our wrap party, I sent Scott a message, updating him on the status of our shoot, and expressing once again, how honored I was to work with him. He replied, "Well, I appreciate the feeling, but you did what so few do—you went ahead and made a movie from your heart. It will pay off many times over."

Yes, I dared to have noble ambitions,
to create a brighter future,
to dream and to achieve my dream, knowing
no man or women can stop me,
*No, not here!**

*From the book *Pomegranate*

Part II

THE PRESENT

Chapter 7

THE HEALING LODGE

At noon, my friend Sonya arrived at our house just as the paramedics carried my mother out on a stretcher. We scheduled this time to work on the yearly spiritual and writing retreat coming up later that year in October, called Path of Consciousness. Sonya had offered to help with the administrative work, and I was glad she was there at that very moment to get my mind off of things.

"I'm going to ride in the ambulance with Mom," said my sister Heyam. "I'll call you from the hospital."

"Okay," I said, not really having a choice in the matter.

She rushed outside where snow caked the tree branches out front. Sonya and I went into my office, otherwise known as "Weam's room" or "Mom's room." She sat at my desk to work on my computer, and I sat on the accent pattern rug over the hardwood floor to sort out the files I had neglected to organize for months now. This helped calm my mind and avoid the reality that my mother was dying. The day I'd been dreading had arrived.

It all started a little over two weeks prior, on Sunday, January 20, 2019, when my family and I returned from an eight-day cruise trip on the Harmony of the Seas. Our group of nineteen people which consisted of relatives and friends, had a great time hopping from the Bahamas to Jamaica to Haiti to Mexico, indulging in all-you-can-eat restaurants, dancing the night away, and in the case of the women, getting thin Jamaican braids and tropical island dresses. We laughed so hard our stomachs hurt, like the time one of my sisters-in-law tried to hand money to an old Jamaican man with raggedy clothes and a cane, assuming he was homeless. He went off on her, gave her a piece of his mind. "Did I ask you for money? Did I?"

Despite the fun, the food, the sun, we were all ready to return home to our daily routine. We arrived at Metro Airport around midnight, and while waiting for our luggage, I called Heyam to ask about Mom. Mom stayed with her whenever I went out of town. Heyam said, "She's lethargic and her left hand is blue."

I thought nothing of it. Mom loved her home and when she was away from it for too long, which was hardly ever, her system would partly shut down. Once home, she would revive. Still, I offered Heyam to go to their house and check on Mom, but she said, "It's late, and we're going to sleep. It's best you go home and rest."

At home, I started unpacking, fell asleep in the middle of the night, then woke up at six in the morning and continued to unpack. I did one load of laundry, got caught up with some of the important emails, then went to Kroger and the Middle Eastern market to shop for groceries. I stopped at Verizon to see if they could fix my daughter's phone which had suddenly died in Haiti. The representative said it had water damage. Then I called my brother and told him to meet me at Heyam's at noon to help me pick up Mom.

When we arrived at Heyam's house, Mom was sitting at the kitchen table. I kissed her and asked how she was doing.

"I'm not good," she said.

She didn't look good, but I'd seen that look before. What shocked me was her left hand. It was blue and shriveled up, Dry. Cold. Dead. The next thing I knew, Adnan was driving her to the ER, and I followed to take over. The tests showed that she had blood clots in her left arm. The doctors said they had to operate immediately. Otherwise, they'd have to amputate her arm.

For the next two weeks, I was on an emotional roller coaster and a chaotic schedule. In the mornings, I dropped off my kids at school, then drove to the hospital. I bought a coffee from the Starbucks on the first floor, took the elevator to my mom's room, and stayed there working on my laptop until I had to pick up the kids up from school. During that time, I journaled a lot, reflecting on the feelings I experienced on the cruise and the timing of my mother's blood clot. Mom always waited for a major project to be done, such as a book, my wedding, or for me to return from a long trip, before she attended to her needs. She got her U.S. citizenship after every one of her children did, and she ate her meals after all her kids had eaten. At the same time, it seemed these needs were always attached to me like a tail on an alligator. I would feel guilty when things went wrong: *Could I have done better? Should we not have agreed to the second procedure which caused her to lose her voice?* I cringe every time I think of the surgeon telling me how she resisted the endotracheal tube that went down her throat.

When I was on Harmony of the Seas, looking deeply into the waves of the ocean, should I not have wondered how I could continue working as hard as I do at home, as a caregiver, mother, and wife, and simultaneously make my dreams a reality? Did this question reach my mother's intuition, leading her to decide that it was time to depart this earth? Or did my absence make it easier for her to free both of us from our physical and psychological bondage? Before I took my mother to live with us, the doctor had said that, given her heart condition, she would not survive more than a year. Nearly five years later, she looked healthier and happier than when the doctor gave his diagnosis.

Heyam said that Mom had behaved differently than other times she'd stayed by her. She slept more than usual, was quite weak, and didn't care to eat. Heyam had set her wheelchair in front of the slightly open slide door in the kitchen so she could get some fresh air. She covered her with a blanket. Mom stared outside for a long while. Unlike before, she didn't ask my sister to place her back on the couch or say she was tired. At night, Heyam laid my mom on the couch and sat on a low sitting stool beside her. She massaged her blue hand to help the blood flow. "Enough, daughter, go rest," she told Heyam.

"No, I'm okay," Heyam assured her.

When Mom's health improved a little, I was eager to take her home and return to the routine that we'd established when she moved in with us nearly five years ago. I'd given up many things in my life for her, and I didn't regret that one bit. Her presence helped me learn more about compassion, aging, death, and to focus on what's important—God, family, writing. It was good for my children too.

Mom and I became inseparable and very, very close. Yes, she often woke me in the middle of the night, thinking it was morning, and yes, she needed care and support at all hours. Sure, I was very tired and it felt as though I had to put my dreams on hold to attend to her twenty-four hours a day. But I prided myself on being good at what I did as a daughter, mother, wife, and caregiver who kept her away from hospitals for almost three years. I learned quite a bit from her doctors and nurses that came in and out of my home, sat at my kitchen table, drank chai and ate *kleicha* (Iraqi cookies), and sometimes even stayed for whatever lunch or dinner I was cooking at the time. I served them food as if they were family and together, we enjoyed Mom's company, personality, stories, and her tricks.

Once, for instance, she called me and said, "Ameera, I can't eat this. It's too salty."

I looked at her bowl, which she'd emptied of the red rice, chicken, and salad I'd served her. I stared at her, dumbfounded. She stared back with innocence until she could no longer hold herself and cracked a mischievous smile.

Ameera means princess and it was her sister's name, the only sister still alive. She lived less than a mile from our home. Mom had two other sisters who had passed away; Victoria burned in a fire, leaving behind three young sons; the other, Katrina (known as Katina) died of old age in Baghdad. Only on a few occasions, when I purposely did not answer for a while to see what she would do, did Mom switch to "Weam! Weam!"

Mom had a Native American nurse with long thin pepper-colored hair that was often put in a bun. Her name was Stella and she'd been trying to retire for ages. Lucky for us, the homecare company she worked for pleaded for her to stay. Loving her job and her patients, she cut her hours to part-time and kept a goal of "soon-to-retire" status. Stella taught me the most. A caregiver of her own mother, she helped me get Mom off the medications that turned her into a zombie. The memory pills made her more forgetful. The bladder control pills caused side effects that required further prescriptions to prevent those problems. I didn't want Mom to eat pills like sunflower seeds, so Stella advised me which medication to throw in the trash, adding, "I'm not supposed to tell you this. I could lose my job…" But then she'd shrug her shoulders, knowing she could trust me and was happy about the idea that soon she'd be retiring.

Mom went from thirteen pills daily to only four: diabetes, aspirin, and two for high blood pressure. Once, a hospital doctor insisted she start using diabetic injections, but Stella and I weaned her off them. For three years, the doctors who made house calls would go over her file and ask what happened to her injections that continued to show on her list of medications. "Oh, Stella and I got her off them. Now I only use those for emergencies. She needs them like twice a year."

"Who's Stella?" they'd ask, confused.

"Her nurse." Or later, "Her former nurse."

They would remain silent, look down at the file, look back up at me, and say, "Okay, so give us a call if you need anything."

In the beginning when I took my mother in, the doctor told me that given her heart condition, she had about a year to live. He was wrong. From Mom's medical team, I learned that when she became lethargic and her sugar count was over four hundred, this was a bladder infection and not to panic. Give her an antibiotic and no, she needn't take them for ten days. Three days were fine and save the rest for the next emergency. This happened twice a year and it literally saved my mom. She celebrated Christmas and New Year's Eve when otherwise she would've spent that special time lying in a hospital. Stella introduced me to an Iranian born physical therapist, Hamed, who was amazing. He bought toys for my kids on Christmas and Easter. Our mother and daughter duo touched many people's hearts. One doctor was in such awe of me taking care of my mother that he kept repeating himself, saying, "It's amazing how you Chaldeans take care of your parents and grandparents."

After two weeks, the hospital discharged my mother. I was relieved. Now she would get better and life would return to normal, I thought. My sister-in-law, Zina, who lives across the street helped me move her from the couch, later to the chair, and at night to the bed. I woke up early Saturday, went to a 7:15 a.m. yoga class and prayed that her healing goes smoothly.

Sunday, I had my sisters, sisters-in-law, mother-in-law, aunt and some cousins come over for lunch. We had a wonderful time and Mom had the chance to eat *dolma* (stuffed grape leaves and other stuffed vegetables). Monday the visiting nurse stopped by. I told her the main problem was Mom not urinating. She placed a catheter, which helped. We changed the dressing for her wounds.

That night, after I fed her *burghul* and some soup, I noticed she had a shortness of breath. She couldn't swallow the last spoons of water and cranberry juice. The pills remained on her tongue until they melted. When I took her to her room, I couldn't carry her to the bed. Her body was loose and heavy with her head, arms, and legs hanging down. None of her muscles held her together. I called Zina for help, and she came immediately. "Why is she breathing like that?" she asked as we carried Mom to the bed.

"I don't know," I said, trying not to panic. I woke up throughout the night checking on her. She kept getting worse, her eyes wide open, her breathing laborious. She didn't sleep an ounce. I felt terrible that there was nothing I could do to give her comfort. The doctor was coming the next morning. I hoped he would somehow have a cure. I didn't want her to end up in the ER and… die at the hospital. I called the nurse at 6:30 a.m. and she said that Mom was probably having kidney failure. She suggested I call 911.

"I was hoping to provide her with hospice care at home," I said, crying.

"That takes time. The doctor has to write an order for hospice care."

My thoughts froze.

"You're a smart woman and will do the right thing," she said.

Once we hung up, I called my sister and told her to come

over right away because I didn't know what to do. I moved a chair and table to Mom's room and sat by her bed, holding her warm hand and reading. Actually, it was more like flipping pages because I couldn't understand the words scattered in front of me like a shattered puzzle. I prayed the doctor would show up and save the day. Mom would wake up, a little grumpy, but alive.

"Would you like some tea?" I asked Sonya, pretending everything was alright.

"Yes, please," she said in her soft and gentle voice.

I went into the kitchen and prepared cardamom tea and served it in my office with a plate of walnuts, dates, and figs. "I have a curry chicken and potato dish for later," I said.

"That sounds delicious."

I returned to sorting out the files. We worked quietly. I called Heyam regularly, asking for updates. Things didn't look good. Mom's blood pressure was low. The doctor discouraged any type of aggressive treatment.

Sonya's energy helped keep me grounded, as did my office which I considered my healing lodge. I have so many precious memories in this room. Suddenly, after giving birth to my daughter, I couldn't go to Caribou Coffee a few miles down from home without it becoming an elaborate affair. All I wanted was to sip a handcrafted caramel coffee while writing and reading at my favorite café, in my favorite spot—near the fireplace in the winter and next to the window in the summer— and sip a handcrafted caramel coffee while writing and reading.

As a single woman, I could simply pick up my bag and laptop and go. As a mother, barriers arose. Someone had to watch my children or else I had to dress their uncooperative little bodies, pack numerous bags, hear myself use profanities

I hadn't used before, and feel an adrenaline rush as I maneuvered myself in and out of places, trying to get the most out of my short free time which didn't feel so free after all. My attempts to reach Caribou Coffee proved excruciating.

Then one day while at the coffee shop, staring ahead, trying to figure out how I would be able to ever write again, I remembered the words of my Native American teacher, Chip. He'd often said, quoting a Chinese proverb, "If you stay long enough in one place, the whole world will pass by." With these words, an image of my home appeared, or more precisely the family room which I'd turned into my writing office and later also privately called "my healing lodge." I could just do my writing there. I created it just for that, to write, and yet in the beginning, I wasn't accustomed to write in it, hence, Caribou Coffee.

It was a spacious room with cherry wood file furniture that included a cabinet, bookshelves, and a desk facing a large window overlooking the backyard. The previous owners of this house, a Polish man and his Chaldean wife, used the room to store items. The couple was in their sixties and had only been married for two years. When the woman learned that I wanted to turn the family room into my writing space, a lovely office with a desk and bookshelves, she suggested to instead use one of the three bedrooms for *that*. I explained I'm a writer. She nodded and reiterated the use of one of the three bedrooms for *that*.

The other rooms, I explained, have windows slightly bigger than a large cardboard box so I wouldn't have as good a view of the outside to see nature unless I sat on a highchair. I'd get claustrophobic and frustrated, not inspired, and inspiration is food for writers. She listened, but not really, and reinstated that this room, intended to be a splendid family room, would be wasted as an office. I said no more, realizing the extent of her ignorance as to the value of a book or a writer. Like myself, she was Chaldean, a descendent of a people known to have invented many things in ancient Mesopotamia, including writing. The first recorded writer in history is Enheduanna, a princess, priestess, and poet from that region. Nonetheless, the truth is I was an oddity, one of few in my community who put a library of books in their home.

This interrogation of *"Why don't you move your office into another room?"* went on with other Chaldeans. A house painter who was painting the entire house couldn't fathom why I'd go to the extreme of occupying a large room which faced the main entrance of my house with a desk and books commanding respect. Like his predecessors, he suggested, as he flapped his hands this way and that way, like a fish flip flopping, "Take the books elsewhere, either to the basement or simply get rid of them."

The idea of moving nearly a thousand books and the shelves they were sitting on, painting, then moving them back into place, absolutely baffled him. His reaction left no opportunity for me to explain that many of these books were classics and as old as a hundred years. Some belonged to my college days, such as *Madame Bovary* and *Washington Square*.

Despite the skeptics, the room today still sits at the center of the house. It has a large window, three and a half walls, and no doors. One shelf serves as an altar with candles, incense, pictures of loved ones, and small items with spiritual significance, some having traveled from as far as India and Tibet; an antique miniature bronze elephant, a colorful hanging peacock, and a meditation bell. A large painting of a grey wolf sits on the floor against the bookshelf. The wolf is in the woods at night, surrounded by snowflakes, and observing you with kind but mysterious eyes that make you feel there's another being in there. Everyone likes that painting. Other shelves contain large feathers gifted by my teacher, Lynn; the mug I bought from Prague where I studied poetry; the beaded tablecloth my sister-in-law brought from Turkey and gifted to me.

Initially, my children had full access to this room and would crawl, later walk and run through the doorway to easily reach a different section of the house. It helped me have eyes in the back of my head as I worked on my computer. Years later, I remodeled it to create a warmer and more literary atmosphere, and to have a slight disconnect from the activities around me by use of a long and short bookcase to block off one of the two entrances.

Even today, when I sit in this room, I'm at my center; I have one foot in the spiritual world. When I step out of the room, I'm cooking, cleaning, or doing other household duties; I have one foot in the physical world. The one foot here, the other foot there gave, and still gives me a balance and serenity that flows into the rest of my home. It takes me into the day's work with an unspoken language, my roots entwined with creativity and the essence of Mother Earth.

One day I drove past my favorite coffee shop and wondered why I hadn't seen it. I enjoyed reminiscing about my early writing days whenever I passed by Caribou Coffee. How did I miss it this time? Was I daydreaming or immersed in the music? Did my eyesight fail me? No, the truth was that Caribou Coffee had turned into a jewelry store. It changed owners, names, and purpose, causing me to experience a short burst of denial followed by melancholy.

Regardless of what occurred on the outside, I stayed in one place, a room, and continued to write years later. That room, centered in the center, was situated in a way that helped me take care of my mother while continuing to write years later. Her wheelchair in the adjacent living room gave her full view access to me, and it gave me full access to her. She'd be watching television and occasionally turn to me. We'd knowingly stare at each other for a while, in an unconditional loving way. Or she would say, "Jesus has risen." I would nod, and she would emphasize, with bright eyes, "Jesus has risen."

I'd look at the television set and see nothing but actors, or even a blank screen, but I knew she saw something else, something that made her radiate with light. About a week or so before we left on the cruise, her eyes were brighter than usual when she suddenly turned to me and said, "Jesus has risen."

"Okay, Mom," I said and continued typing on my computer.

She said it again, with emphasis, and I muttered, "Yeah, that's good."

But she insisted I hear and understand the subtlety behind her words. I looked at her and saw light on her face. She beamed with happiness. I smiled to assure her I was aware of all life, seen and unseen, named and unnamed. She smiled in return, content.

The night before leaving on the trip, my sister Nidhal, who is eleven years my senior, colored and straightened my hair. She even put in a few streaks of highlights. When my mother saw me, she stared in awe. Her eyes sparkled and her wide smile caused lots of wrinkles as she exclaimed in Arabic, "Wow, how beautiful you are!"

I don't remember her ever saying those words to me.

We had found the beauty in each other and wanted to delight in this great gift for as long as possible. We knew our time together was limited, that our days were numbered, that the angels might appear that night or the next morning to take her away to be with her deceased tribe. Our time was precious, fragile, short, and sacred, because it would soon be our last earthly memories of each other.

CHAPTER 8

TOGETHER AGAIN

Once Sonya left, I went to the hospital where I remained for thirty-six hours. Mom's room was crammed with her children, grandchildren, in-laws, cousins, and the nurses that occasionally walked in to check on her. It was like watching the flocks of Canadian geese gathering at the pond behind our home where Mom and I lived before I got married. I'd watch them from the window and marvel at their tribe. Geese mate for life, raise and protect their babies together, and take care of one another. Unlike other birds, they even molt their feathers together. To fly in formation, they work as a team.

Mom observed each person with eyes wide open, like a deer in headlights, due to a medication that made her alert and enabled us to have a few waking hours with her. The nurses waited for us to sign the consent forms to remove her off life support. Some of my siblings couldn't accept this idea so an Arabic doctor came to speak to us. He kindly said in Arabic that he understood our pain, but that keeping Mom alive would just cause her prolonged suffering. I signed, tears dripping on the papers and smearing the ink.

Once the nurses took off Mom's life support, they moved her to another room for hospice patients where exactly the same time last year my father-in-law lay. We followed. More family members arrived and groups began to break up and hang outside in the hallway or waiting room or small kitchen area. They sat on chairs, couches, tables, and formed circles on the floor. Our cousins brought thermoses of tea and coffee, containers of homemade cooking, and trays of catered food that ranged from shawarma and Subway sandwiches to meat and cheese pies.

It so happened that another large Chaldean family's mother was dying in the room next to my mom's. Her name was also Shamamta, a name derived from *shamama* which is a sweet melon known for its pleasant fragrance. It's the size of a baseball and once you hold it, it gives your palms a nice smell. Some people even use it in their home as an aroma freshener. At the beginning of its growth, it is green. Over time, orange and brown stripes form on its outer cover due to the sun's rays. The fruit saturates the market back home in the summer. It has various health benefits and a special place in literature where poets such as Rumi have written about the importance of this fruit, also known as sweet tiger melon in English and *dastanbo* in Persian. In India, the word shamama refers to a unique essential oil.

The relatives of the other Shamamta had set up their food trays, food containers, and thermoses in a separate but nearby section. They offered my son and his cousin meat pies when they saw them sitting around a table, their faces in their hands to cover their tears. My son and cousin took the meat pies and continued to cry.

"Mom, I think she's gone," one of my nephews said to his mom as he stood over my mother's bed.

Up until that moment, I was fairly calm, cool, and collected. I'd only showed my sorrow when my daughter arrived at the hospital and fell into my embrace. We both wept an agonizing cry. But when I heard "she's gone" I suddenly became frantic, broke down, and sobbed, "No, I don't want her to go! I don't want her to go!"

My sisters and other family members tried to calm me down and I heard them say along with the nurses, "She's still here. She's not gone yet."

"But she *is going,* and I don't want her to go! I was so happy that she lived with us!" I cried in Arabic, releasing the fears, sadness, and tears that had been wrapped up as tightly as a newborn's swaddle. A cousin embraced me like a blanket, making me feel warm and safe while the child in me came to terms with the fact that Mom was not immortal, even though for years I watched her slipping away. I never imagined it would be this particular cousin who would offer such support, although thirty years ago, I was her maid-of-honor and our tribes are connected in so many ways.

The hour grew late, and people started to leave. The last to go were my siblings. They left slowly, reluctantly, knowing this would be the last time they would see Mom alive. For the second night, my sister Nidhal stayed with me. She offered the croissant and yogurt she'd brought from home. I shook my head and said, "I'm not hungry." One of my sisters-in-law came late and left around 2:30 a.m. We then decided to go to sleep. The nurse said she'd reserved an empty room for us a few doors down. It had two beds, a TV, and a bathroom. It looked like a pleasant hotel room.

"What's the use of staying with Mom if we're not going to be beside her at her last moment?" Nidhal asked.

"We can alternate," I said, thinking the same thing.

"That's a good idea." She suggested I go to the room first, so I gathered my books and laptop. I laid on the bed for about five minutes, then gathered my things again and returned to Mom's room.

"It feels lonely in there," I said. "I want to be by Mom."

"Me too."

Nidhal slept on the couch by the window and I curled up

on the chair beside Mom's bed. Though drowsy, my eyes stayed awake. I observed her hands, swollen with smooth pink skin and green fingertips that looked like someone painted them with green nail polish. I periodically held her hand and I listened to her breaths which were full of air but grew few and far in between. Each time there was a pause in her breath, my sister would jump off the couch and rush to Mom's side. She'd see the breathing continue after a long moment and return to the couch. This happened three or four times. Then there was a sudden change, a softness, a surrender in the breathing.

"Nidhal," I called out quietly, knowingly.

She leapt and made it in time to witness Mom's third and last breath at 5:40 a.m., documented 5:45 a.m. by the nurses. It took them a few minutes to come in, listen for a heartbeat, and pronounce her dead. Before the break of dawn, my sister wept in the dark for the loss of a woman that became no more, turning into a flowing stream, dancing into thin air, traveling into the stars and moon. I numbly thought of those last three breaths that were as sweet as honey and as sharp as the edge of a knife. Those last three breaths that peeled my mother from this earth and garnished the universe with her spirit.

Before sunrise, my siblings arrived and surrounded my mom's bed in an oval shape. Each expressed their own grief and took turns sitting closest beside her. We examined her lifeless body, and some commented on her soft and white skin that was free from the blemishes or bruises caused by aging. Her belly had a high roundness that resulted from carrying and birthing twelve children. It barely had any stretch marks. One brother aggravatingly told his twin brother to move along and give others a turn. He was the older twin, by a minute or two, and always ordered the younger one around. One of my sisters cried that now that Mom was gone, we would never gather like we did before. She loved hosting family and visiting their homes. The nurse came to roll Mom's bed out so she could be transported to the mortuary. She warmly assured us that Mom would always be with us and asked if we had any last instructions for them. We asked that the morticians not remove the wooden beaded cross she wore around her neck.

Later that same day, the other Shamamta also passed away. That night we held a prayer vigil at Holy Martyr's church hall and hundreds of people dressed in black showed up. Large flowers and tables of plentiful food appeared, ordered and prepared by I don't know who. Men sat on one side, the women on the other. The closest relatives, including myself, sat on chairs facing everyone. Hundreds of people walked by before leaving to touch our hands, or kiss our heads, and offer condolences. The women's side usually has an elderly woman intensifying the grief by sharing stories about the deceased in a sorrowful though poetic voice. In the past, some have even hired a professional to ululate. This wailing helped bring to surface a deep anguish where some women pulled their hair and beat their heads or hearts to show love and respect for the deceased. This practice has diminished over time.

Three days after Mom passed away, the closest women in the family—sisters, sisters-in-law, and my aunt—visited the gravesite to light candles and burn incense, representing Jesus' triumph over death on the third day. It took us a while to find her grave with the inches of snow that had piled up. The women then came to my home for brunch. During this period, people who come to the deceased's home are only *supposed to* be served bitter coffee and tea with no sugar, representing the state of the household. Of course, rarely anyone exercised that tradition anymore. A similar practice is used in Switzerland, where male mourners place lemon rinds on the grave after the funeral service to symbolize the sharpness of their grief.

At this time, I was numb with grief. I went through the

motions necessary to attend the funeral, make decisions about the burial, and take care of my home and kids. I waited for my mother to come and nourish my broken heart with a word of encouragement, guidance, something. I just wanted to hear her voice, to see her, even if in my dreams. But my sorrow was like a great heavy wall that blocked the energy from coming. I remembered my cousin's husband, who was also related to my mother. The night Mom passed away, when we went to pick up our children from his home, he slowly walked to the car, to my window, a cigarette in his hand. He said, "Your mother is watching you, and she will feel sad to see you in this condition."

He had been at the hospital when I broke down. In the past, we'd barely shared more than two words with each other. Plus, his wife and I weren't on the best of terms. But much had happened within forty-eight hours. While family members and hospice nurses bustled in and out, creating the chaos and stir that goes with life, deeper kinships were developing with our relatives. We emptied ourselves of past grudges and resentments, all which now seemed petty and trivial. A shift crawled into our consciousness, aligning and adapting our energies with the afterworld that embodied my mother's consciousness.

I decided to write a letter.

Dear Mom,

Two weeks ago, we buried you and I no longer could share my mornings and nights with you. Your absence has left much emptiness, such a void, and I'm afraid to talk about it, to confirm it is true. You are gone. After all these years of having such a powerful presence in my life, you have moved on to a restful place where you won't have the physical limitations you had here.

I miss you so much… I loved having you in my home. I loved taking care of you even when it exhausted me. It was so well worth it and you showered me with so many gifts and blessings when you were here. It feels strange to communicate to you in this way, through paper, through spirit, knowing I can't go home and hug and kiss you goodnight before I put you to bed. Thank you for going slowly, for weaning out of the physical life, for helping us stand firmly before leaving us. Thank you for all the teachings, the love, the stability you gave.

I know that no matter how long I had you I would not have had enough. Something about your presence was so comforting. Often, I wished I could bring in a twenty-four-hour caregiver so I could just enjoy your company without the work. But now that you're gone, I'm honored to have had served you in this way. I learned so much about you, serving, healing, faith and God, in the process. I'm so grateful to you.

About two weeks later, I dreamt I was in a room with my sister and my mom lying there. She's not looking too good, is comatose. But after a while she starts being alert. I want to say to my sister, "Didn't Mom already die? Didn't we bury her?" I remember the burial when the casket was lowered into the ground and calling the Social Security office to tell them she was gone. How was I going to explain this to the Social Security people? If only I hadn't called them so quickly.

Mom starts looking even better and says, "I'm hungry. I want to eat."

I rush to get her something and see it has already been ordered. A woman walks in with a food pushcart.

Within a month of her death, I had three dreams where I discovered Mom is not dead. But I was dead inside, dull, half-asleep, and needed to wake up, to become once again bold, assertive, energetic, and full of determination. Oh, where was Scarlett O'Hara when you needed her? When hardships called, she made do with the sources at hand, showing up in front of

Rhett Butler with the green curtain dress made by her mammy. If things got in her way, she nipped them in the bud with an impatient, "Fiddle-dee-dee!" and "Great balls of fire, don't bother me anymore, and don't call me sugar!"

Two months later, on my daughter's thirteenth birthday in April, I attended an information session at 8:15 a.m. in a Detroit café with Adam Ganuza from the Knight Foundation about a grant for one of my projects. My sister Heyam joined me so that afterward we could drive to Holy Sepulcher Cemetery to meet with Nibras from the funeral home. We were going to exhume my father's vault and move it next to my mother's grave at White Chapel Memorial Park Cemetery.

The group of five to six men had already started digging Dad's grave by the time we arrived. One woman, an administrator at the cemetery, stood beside them. It was another hour before the truck lifted the coffin vault. My sister and I stood a little distance away, watching, chatting, reminiscing, and often holding back tears. Heyam was cold. She hadn't dressed warm enough for the weather. I offered my gloves more than once, but she refused to take them. Nibras came to check on us every now and then. I had several calls with my niece, Cassandra, who was watching Teddy, the new member of our family who arrived to our home three days prior.

Nibras said if anything breaks from the vault, not to be scared. We became emotional but kept it together, our hearts beating fast. He joined the men once again. Loud hammering sounds made us fear the worst. The vault might tip over, drop, crack, even cause a skeleton to pop out.

The phone rang. It was the translation company I worked for. I stared at the phone, my sister looking at it as well. That same moment, as I tried to accept the call, Nibras approached me, and the coffin lifted out of the grave. I felt suspended in air, as if Babba was telling me not to waste time with meaningless things. I understood and let the call go. The translation company then tried calling my sister, but her phone was on mute, so she didn't see it until hours later. It didn't go past us that over fifty years ago, one of my father's side jobs was a translator. I still have his two English-Arabic dictionaries, so old and thick that their binding is Duct taped; one, with a brownish cover, is titled Elias' Modern Dictionary (816 pages), nineteenth edition, published in Cairo in 1974; the other, with the red cover, is titled Al-Mawrid Modern Dictionary (1090 pages), second edition, published in Lebanon in 1969.

Nibras gave me a small hug of support and stood beside us for a while. "They're going to make a hole in the vault to drain the water," he said. "The men don't want you to see that."

The woman came toward us, tears in her eyes, and embraced us. "It's nice that he'll be next to Mamma now."

I wept. My sister and I had fought for this, especially me, because I'd promised Mom. When her sealed vault was lowered into the grounds of White Chapel, while the women around me wailed and screamed, to the sight of everyone dressed in complete black, I said loudly, clearly, and repeatedly that we would bring Babba beside her. Those words, along with the tears, were absorbed by the earth. It was a done deal.

Thirty-three years ago, we buried my father, my Babba, at Holy Sepulcher Cemetery where the majority of Chaldeans buried their loved ones. The Catholic cemetery consists of about 350 acres of land and dates back to 1928. It is situated on beautiful, forested grounds near Lake Geneserath, home to birds and waterfowl such as geese, ducks, and even an occasional blue heron or egret. Many monuments and private family mausoleums herald the names of prominent individuals such as politicians, leaders of the Archdiocese of Detroit, clergymen, veterans, etc.

Located in Southfield, Michigan, it takes about thirty

minutes to drive there from Sterling Heights, and for most Chaldeans, that's like traveling to the moon. So in the thirty-three years of my father being buried there, we visited him once on Father's Day. We searched for the gravesite as if doing an Easter egg hunt, the women dressed in black. I ended up finding the slab, buried beneath grass and dirt. We cleaned it up and sat there in sadness. While our mother lived, we felt our father's presence through her. Now that she was gone, we needed him closer to home.

Over time, Chaldeans who lived on the East Side, the Little Baghdad-ers, began to choose a different cemetery, one more accessible. The family had no doubt that we would bury my mom at White Chapel, but some saw the process of relocating Babba's casket a bad luck omen. The funeral director said that the Chaldean diocese recently moved the nuns' graves because they didn't have enough space in one area and wanted them kept together. The same people who considered it a bad luck omen now said the process was unnecessary. They didn't believe in cemeteries and wouldn't visit anyway. Well, if they didn't believe in cemeteries, why did they believe in bad omens? And why stop those who did believe in cemeteries and wanted to visit?

"The presence or absence of a body is irrelevant," someone said. "It's the memories, not the cold stone that counts." True, but this was an ancient tradition that honors the dead. The Sumerians of Mesopotamia believed in an afterlife under the earth five thousand years ago so they buried their dead and others followed suit. And Chaldeans celebrate the Day of the Dead, which is observed by the Roman Catholic Church.

Some of us believed that money was the only reason the others pushed back. The ones that wanted Babba moved were willing to pay for it. I was willing to pay extra. This was our last gift to Mom, and our first major gift to Babba, who I never had the chance to gift anything to except for naming my publishing company after him. Hermiz, derived from the Persian Hormizd, was the name of a Chaldean saint from the seventh century. In Greek mythology Hermes was known as the messenger of the gods and his name appears twice in the Bible. It is thought that he was probably a pre-Hellenic god who existed as a Mesopotamian snake-god, serving as a mediator between humans and the divine, especially Ishtar.

Plus I couldn't bear the idea of my mom being there all alone when all her life she had been surrounded by a tribe. Furthermore, what about her husband, the man she had twelve children with? How would we pay our respect to him as our father and share stories of him with our children? How could we visit Mom and ignore Dad? What about his life and memories? I imagined sometimes taking a chair and sitting at my parents' headstone to read, journal, or just enjoy the peaceful quiet. After some convincing, the few who hesitated to move Babba's coffin signed the necessary forms for the city to give the funeral home a burial transit permit.

The men placed the heavy headstone in my trunk. I noticed my father's name in English and Arabic, with the surname Maria engraved only in Arabic. Now, there was excitement in the air as my sister and I got in the car and drove away.

"We got Babba out of there," Heyam said, thrilled.

"We did it!" I said, giving her a high five. "We brought Babba next to Mamma, to where we all live, where we will visit him every time we visit her."

Before we drove away, we decided to park on the side, step out of the car, and take a stroll along the beautiful large trees and maintained grounds. We wanted to see if we recognized any of the Chaldean names on the opulent headstones and ornate statues. Some had benches beside them. We considered the destruction of the centuries-old cemetery of Tel

Keppe, located on a hill behind the main church, where our grandparents and many relatives had been buried. ISIS bulldozed their way through it, smashing headstones, damaging monuments. They forbade anyone from visiting the graves, which they viewed as a pagan practice. They dug up every grave in search of gold, rings, necklaces, or whatever jewelry they could find, and left random bones and clothes scattered everywhere. Years later, parts of the rubble have been cleared and the entrance to the cemetery repaired. The cross that stood at its gate for centuries was carefully restored and re-erected.

The fate of Maria Theresa Asmar's burial site comes to mind. She was born in Tel Keppe in 1804, and during the Ottoman Empire, witnessed the martyrdom of her family due to their Christian faith. She traveled alone to Europe and the Middle East and published in English a two-part memoir series called *Memoirs of a Babylonian Princess*. Maria is said to have died in France in 1870, although some, including Emily Porter who researched and wrote extensively about her life, believe she died in Tel Keppe. In her will, Maria left a portion of her wealth to restore the church in Tel Keppe and requested that she be buried in the churchyard. Her grave is believed to be there. If so, I as well as she, I'm sure, can't bear the thought of how badly extremists have ravaged it.

Another sister, Awatif, met us at the cemetery, Babba's new home. We stood together and watched as they lowered his casket next to Mom's, like a bride watching her groom walk down the aisle rather than the other way around. We felt the opposite of what we had felt earlier. We were happy and celebratory. This was a very special moment. We'd brought our parents together. We imagined the day of their wedding, the honeymoon phase that followed, their days of joy when their first child, George, was born, and their grief when he died. Their ups and downs as they had eleven more children, as they went from various economic hardships, the emigration process, their loss of each other. They had spent over forty years together on this earth, and they'll stay together, even if just symbolically. Like Scarlett, their daughters had, and continued to have gumption, the bravery, to fight for their own morals and follow their dreams, and at the same time, to attend to their duties.

I'm reminded of an Egyptian Arabic song by Fayza Ahmad called *Set El Habayeb*, the *Master of the Beloved Ones*. It's quite old, a classic, but it's still the most popular Mother's Day song with lyrics that bring before the eyes of any child, a mother's love and compassion.

Oh sweet one, you are filled with kindness
You have long stayed up, and toiled to spare me long sleepless nights,
And even today, you still carry the burdens I'm supposed to carry.
I sleep and you stay up, consumed by your thoughts
And you arise with the break of dawn to come check on me.
May you live long for my sake, my love, my mother.
My soul is but a piece of your soul, and I thrive only because of your silent prayers.
If I were to spend a lifetime trying to repay your precious deeds,
From where would I find the most precious gift?

CHAPTER 9

TEDDY BEAR

"Did Teddy change your life?" my husband asked my son.

"Yes," my son responded.

"Did he change Mamma's life?"

"Yes, a lot."

My husband agreed with my son, and so did I, but I didn't voice my agreement. I simply listened to them converse as I sat on the floor next to the wood-burning fireplace and watched the flames. On the hearth laid a mug of cocoa, books, laptop, journal, and pens and pencils. My favorite way to end a cold winter night. Teddy, our Shih Tzu, often sat beside me, enjoying, like the rest of us, the calm, soothing, and meditative feeling this atmosphere brought forth. I had known nothing about Shih Tzus until after I fell in love with Teddy, the doll I never got, who made me feel like a little girl.

I grew up not having pets, or for that matter, toys. On top of that, we didn't exchange gifts for Christmas or celebrate birthdays. I once did receive a gift in Baghdad from my brother who lived in America; a large, gorgeous, and colorful doll that was almost my height. But I was told to wait until we got to America for me to play with it. It remained covered in thick plastic wrapping. I never got to touch or hold it, and I don't recall ever seeing it again.

Not all people in the Arab world celebrate birthdays. In fact, some don't even know what day they were born.

Registering births, marriages, and deaths was an un-ripened process. In 1957, in an effort to take a census for the first time, the Iraqi government decided to register all children that did not own IDs. They chose July 1st to be their birth date; it was only the year that they attempted to get right. It's estimated that at least a third of Iraq's seniors share that birthday. They never imagined the predicament that might surface as a result. For instance, when one day, a local gas station offered free gas for people whose birthday was on July 1st, they did not expect to see a line of cars form all the way down the street.

There are also Christian sects that do not celebrate birthdays. Jehovah's Witnesses refrain from this custom due to its pagan origins and its connections to magic and superstitions; birthday candles, in folk belief, are endowed with special magic for granting wishes. While the Bible does not forbid birthdays, it condemns the use of magic, divination, spiritism, or anything like that. Jehovah's Witnesses argue that one reason why God condemned the ancient city of Babylon is because its inhabitants practiced astrology, a form of divination.

Some Muslim clerics see celebrating birthdays as adopting a non-Muslim culture. They refer to a *Hadith*, a collection of traditions containing sayings of Prophet Muhammad, that says, "Whoever imitates people (in their actions) is one of them." They denounce birthdays, citing the Hadith which states that "The most evil affairs are the innovations, and every innovation is an error." Other clerics stay neutral, relying on Quran verses that favor freedom, such as "God gave humankind the intellect and ability to discern between right and wrong."

Evidently, interpretations of holy texts and subsequent opinions can alter long-standing cultural traditions.

The warmth and crackling and popping noises from the fire continued to tranquilize the house. Teddy cuddled closer to me, and I put my writing tools down and began to pet his soft luxurious coat. He rolled over on his back and offered his tummy, indicating for me to give him a belly rub. I obeyed, smiling. I've learned so much about Shih Tzus since he came into our home. I had no idea that they come in so many different shapes and sizes. Teddy is a purebred Shih Tzu with the official color of silver (closest to white) and liver (chocolate). There are eight types of Shih Tzus that stem from the same breed, and someone once told me that mine is an American Shih Tzu because of his physical attributes that include a small chest, high and forward-facing and frontal shoulders, a short neck, square-shaped head, and small wide set eyes.

People commonly associate the Shih Tzu with China, but they actually came from China's western neighbor, Tibet, which was a sovereign nation until the 1950s. The Chinese then bred them with Pekingese or Pugs to create the modern-day Shih Tzu. They were originally bred to sit around the palace of the Emperor of China and bark when people or animals approached to alert guards to the presence of unwanted visitors. But soon they became a favorite of the Imperial Chinese court as companion dogs rather than working dogs.

Although the Chinese name Shih Tzu translates to "little lion," there is nothing fierce about this adorable dog breed. In fact, these pooches are lovers and not hunters. The affectionate and happy dogs are outgoing and love nothing more than to follow their people around the home. They have made themselves comfortable on the laps of humans from various walks of life for centuries. However, in recent years, they have become less lap dogs and more active dogs as their parents train them in dog sports, obedience, rally, and agility competitions.

With the tip of my finger, I wiped away a few hot chocolate

stains off the hearth. Then I observed the coziness of the room and reflected on what people call "chance" or "destiny." Teddy was planned as well as unplanned, but he was definitely destined to be in our home. My daughter's thirteenth birthday was two months after my mother's death, and since the time we were on the cruise, she kept mentioning "the promise" to get a dog for her birthday which I could not remember ever making. Her younger brother cheered her on. "Yes, Mom, you promised! We want a dog!"

But I didn't want a dog anymore, or any living thing to come into my house for me to take care of, and then endure having to lose it. I was depressed and tired and I wanted to wallow in my misery—to listen all day to the Chaldean hymns that we played at my mother's death bed and funeral. Can't a woman grieve in peace? Besides, the reason I wanted a dog for half-a-second was because I had heard dogs were linked to positive child development and they had healing powers for the sick and elderly. The second part was gone. My mom was dead. Why bother?

Seeing my unresponsiveness, my husband assured the kids that he'd take matters into his own hands and get them the dog they wanted. "Yeah!" they applauded, and I froze. The thought terrified me! If my husband took the reins, God only knows what would enter through our door. A bear or fox, maybe even a crocodile. Whatever the animal, I'd have to train it and look after it, so I had to save the day.

Grudgingly, I wore my cape, I mean coat, gathered my misery into my purse and carried it with me as we went shopping for a dog. I had a new mission. Naturally, the family got involved. My sister-in-law found a Shih Tzu on Facebook. He looked a little shabby and sad, not cute and cuddly. I contacted the owner, nevertheless. She messaged me, "Meet my brother at the restaurant where he works. It's his dog. He'll have the dog there." After messaging back and forth to schedule a time that worked for both of us, I received a text just as we drove into the parking lot that the dog was already sold.

"But we just messaged you ten minutes ago that we're coming, and you said that he was waiting for us," I wrote.

"I know! I'm so sorry! It's sold."

My children began to whine, and I told them to be patient. "This dog wasn't meant for us. This whole thing was shady. The girl cancels last minute, and her brother gets to bring a dog inside a restaurant?"

My husband agreed. "Babba, you have to understand that this is a *nafas*. It's not a simple matter. The one who enters our home will be the one meant for us."

The Arabic word *nafas* has several meanings. It means "breath" as in breathing or soul or self. The children, of course, didn't understand their father's message, not because of its Arabic word. They simply believed parents should attend to their children's wants and desires as quickly and easily as the genie did for Aladdin.

The next stop was a pet store in a mall. There, we met all types of dog breeds. There were playpens where the kids could interact with the dog to see how they got along. The worker placed one adorable tiny puppy in the playpen. He caught the kids off guard with his sudden viciousness and longing to bite. The kids screamed and struggled to exit the playpen. One dog was cute but refused to move let alone play. "He's sleepy," the worker said. She then brought a shabby little Shih Tzu that captured the kids' hearts. When my husband learned of the price attached to him, he bellowed, "We can buy a car for that much!" Realistically, we couldn't. Well, not a decent car, at least. But I did agree that the Shih Tzu was pricey, and I told the kids we'd keep looking. They kept complaining.

That night I found a Shih Tzu on a website given to me by

a teacher I met the year before at a white elephant Christmas party. She said they had initially bought a dog to help her teenage son through some emotional trouble. The dog ended up changing the life of the entire family, especially hers. The children accused her of loving the dog more than them, and she proudly couldn't deny it. She placed his picture on her iPhone screen, gave him whatever he so desired, and talked about him with bright sparkling eyes, as though he was the most wonderful thing that ever happened to her.

The Shih Tzu, twelve-weeks-old, was the last of five siblings, and as white as snow with brown streaks on his back. Something about him felt perfect. I called the breeder and learned she was an Albanian grandmother who lived in a nearby neighborhood. The details of his groomer caused me to feel a deeper connection to the puppy.

On a cold April morning, two days before my daughter's thirteenth birthday and my father's fault exhumation, I drove to the Albanian grandmother's house with my children. We walked in with curiosity and eagerness, and we walked out with a four-pound new addition to the family. In the car, the puppy, temporarily named Mario, sat on my son's lap. My daughter named him Teddy and my son gave him the middle name Bear, and said to him, "I promise I will take good care of you."

My nieces and nephew from across the street saw us coming with the puppy and hurried over to meet him. Inside, they placed him on my mom's old floral blanket and went goo-goo and ga-ga over him. They promised him all sorts of things, like they would play with him, take him out, feed him, and the list went on. But Teddy became Mamma's boy. He depended on me for food, drink, cleaning after his messes, and taking him on daily walks. He followed me everywhere. Sometimes I would be sitting at my desk, engrossed in my computer task or in the memories of my recently departed mother, and when I got up to refill my coffee cup, I'd accidently step on his paw or tail. He'd jump and I'd realize we have a new family member that could easily be mistaken for a stuffed animal. Within days, I began to shift slightly out of my grief.

Then it happened. I heard myself laughing. I was mopping the floor the primitive way—before mops were invented—by using a towel and bending over in what yoga instructors call downward facing dog posture. Teddy rushed over and grabbed one end of the towel and pulled it with his teeth. "No, Teddy! No!" I said pulling it away. He refused to let go. Even when I raised the towel up high, he clung tight with his teeth and dangled from it like it was a ride in a carnival, a Ferris wheel perhaps.

I succumbed to him and resumed mopping while his teeth clutched onto the towel. My movement caused him to swerve to the left, then swerve to the right, his stomach slipping and sliding on the wet kitchen tile floor, reminding me of the inflatable water slide we'd once bought for the kids. The scene made me laugh, then laugh harder and harder, especially when his strength beat mine and he ran off with the towel in victory and hid in my office. Hearing myself laugh, I realized this was the first time I had laughed in months, since before my mother died. This confirmed what I had suspected shortly after Teddy entered our home—he would help heal my sorrow.

As I continued to wait for signs from Mom, Teddy's shenanigans lifted my spirits. Cleaning after his mess and potty training him kept my mind busy. At Partridge Creek, what we call the "Doggy Mall," a perfectly landscaped outdoor mall where people brought their dogs, Teddy grabbed countless peoples' attention. They stopped and asked to pet him, called him "cute" and a "peanut." Dog owners gave me all sorts of advice, on potty training, protecting Teddy when big dogs passed by, how to get him to sleep through the night. We bought a potty-training DVD with a doggie doorbell.

It didn't take too long for Teddy to start ringing the bell to go out to take care of personal business, or whenever he wanted to get fresh air, chase a cat or squirrel, or simply gaze at the stars. He kept me busy with his needs, warmed up my heart with his love, and effortlessly made me laugh. He restored my joy as I entered a lighthearted, comical, fuzzy world that resembled the land of children's books.

During this time, large monarch butterflies began to appear whenever I was in utter gloom. Their bright orange color, prominent black abstract and line markings with white spots on the edges, brightened my mood. I'd watch a butterfly glide over flowers, or simply flutter in my space, staying long enough for me to see its beauty and understand its message. I felt Mom was communicating to me through the butterfly, telling me she is now happy and free to roam the world, and encouraging me to be hopeful because change and transformation were in the air. Once, I was stuck in traffic when the butterfly appeared on my dashboard. It floated there for what seemed like eternity before it went to a nearby flower bush where it remained, as did the traffic, for at least five minutes.

I knew that my parents were both happy to see me fall completely in love with Teddy, even though he didn't respect the personal space of cats, birds, squirrels, or that of his family's. He insisted on removing my socks from my feet and running outside to bury them in the dirt or snow. He did the same with shoes and shirts, and once he even ran off with my bra and underwear which he stole from the laundry basket. He treated the world like one big toilet and in the beginning, he treated animal waste like a gourmet meal. He arrived at the front door barking long before we could peel ourselves from the living room sofa. He could kill little creatures even though a toothpick was sharper than his teeth and his paw was as soft as cotton. Once when a baby bird fell in our backyard, Teddy tried to catch it with his paw, disorienting the poor bird until the neighbor and I came running out to shoo Teddy away. Teddy was also very discriminatory. He cuddled up to children and women and barked at men, except for the men in the family.

Despite all his little quirks, admittingly, I put him on a pedestal above human beings simply for being a dog. Who would've thought that I would be in love with a dog, and that this dog would change my life? As a child, I was twice chased by dogs in the streets —once in Baghdad by a stray dog and once in Michigan by a Komondor. Neither time did the dogs bite me, but nevertheless, the fear of them remained. Where I came from, keeping animals as pets was not the norm. Usually, if a person had an animal, it was there temporarily to be slaughtered and eaten later, like lamb or chicken, or to be milked or supply eggs on a farm.

While the Quran promotes compassion toward animals, and Muslims are allowed to keep pets like cats and birds, dogs are considered unclean. They should only be kept as guard dogs and hunting dogs because Muhammad said, "The angels do not enter a house in which there is a dog." A website on Islam goes as far as saying that while nonbelievers, Jews, Christians, and communists keep dogs as pets, for Muslims to do so is a sin. The website claims that even if the owner were to clean the dog with the water of all the seas in the world and all the soap in the world, it would never become pure because its impurity is inherent.

The 1979 Islamic Revolution changed many aspects of life for Iranians and their dogs. In the summer of 2022, police there announced that walking dogs in parks was a crime and sought to bring forth new bills to ban the ownership of dogs and other pets because it's a symbol of "Westernization."

Extremists have gone as far as giving out death threats in 2014 for a dog-petting event in Malaysia, which was intended to help people overcome their fear and learn that dogs are also creatures that Allah created who are also in need of love and care. In November of this year, a mayor in Hebron, Palestine offered twenty shekels for every dog killed.

Of course, many Muslims love dogs and even help rescue them. There are great Arab and Persian animal rights activists and charities fighting against such cruelty, but they have an uphill battle on their hands.

Could this abhorrence toward dogs have something to do with the Mesopotamian goddess Gula? Legend has it that after the Great Flood, Gula helped breathe life into mankind. She saw the terrible destruction wrought by the Flood and, since she'd lost her husband to the Netherworld, she became interested in caring for the sick and wounded in the Great Above. She became patroness of herbs, healing, and life. Many ceramic statuettes of her sacred animal, the dog, were dedicated to her at her sanctuaries by people who had been blessed by her. Dogs wandered freely within the sanctuary and played a key role in the healing rituals, although specific details of what they did are unknown. Ceramic dog figures buried at numerous sites, at doorways, and at thresholds were frequently inscribed with Gula's name to protect homes from evil and harm.

The status of female deities began to diminish during the reign of Hammurabi (1792-1750 BC) and afterward, when male gods began to dominate the religious arena. That wasn't the case with Gula, however, whose worship remained with the same respect. Adoration of Gula continued well into the Christian period, and in the Near East Gula was as prevalent as many well-known divinities. Her cult declined little by little until, by the end of the first millennium CE, she had been forgotten.

After Teddy, it seemed to me that the human brain is hard-wired to love dogs, with their floppy ears and big gentle, trusting eyes. Yet they remain a source of fear for many who emigrated from Arab countries, regardless of religion. I'm sure others view my dog as an idiot who has no discipline and barks at the neighbor for no good reason. They wish I would stop doing nothing and start doing something to shut the dog up. Some believe there ought to be an automatic misdemeanor issued when a dog produces noise pollution, in other words, when it barks. A rare few, feeling they live in a dog circus or dog park, believe dog owners should get a dog silencer to avoid that noise pollution. I'm sure these are decent people who have good reasons not to like dogs. Maybe they're afraid of them, have allergies, or some other hang ups. After all, not all dog lovers are good people. Hitler had a German Shepherd named Blondi, and he was a vegetarian.

In our case, Teddy's loyalty and playful nature not only put us in good spirits, but the neighbors as well. After we brought him home, the Chaldean family who lives right behind us, a mother, father, son and daughter, caught Teddy playing in the backyard one day. They were in awe. Teddy cuddled against the fence and stayed there until little by little the family gathered to talk with him, sneaking their fingers through the fence hole to touch him, all along looking around to see if we would be upset by that. I could see them from the window and observed with curiosity where this would end up.

One day, when I was outside, the mother, Ghaida, built up the courage to ask if she could hold Teddy. I said yes and when I gave him to her, her face lit up and the love in her eyes tripled as she held him in her arms. My nine-year-old son didn't particularly like this idea of sharing Teddy. He said, "He's our dog, Mom! He's not their dog!"

"Yes, but they're only holding him. There's nothing wrong with that."

Then the holding evolved into brief visits, just as my son had expected. My son flipped. "Mom, he's our dog, not theirs!"

"Yes, but they can enjoy his company, can't they? You are my son, but you often go to your uncle's house to visit with him and his son. Then after the visit, you return home."

"He's not related to them!"

"He's related by location. They are our neighbors."

This didn't appease my son and as Teddy's visits grew longer, my son's displeasure increased as well.

"Do you love Teddy?" I asked him.

"Of course, I do!"

"Well, Teddy is wanting these visits too, and he's enjoying them as much as the neighbors are. Imagine if we stopped letting you visit your uncle's house because we wanted you all to ourselves. Wouldn't that be selfish? Wouldn't that make you sad?"

He kept pouting, but he understood and soon he learned to share. Years later he too ended up jumping over that fence to play with the neighbor's son.

Teddy created two mammas and two babbas for himself, along with two brothers and two sisters. He had two very happy families. We all watched him with fascination, wondering whether people domesticated dogs or dogs domesticated humans. Dogs can sense how you're feeling. Imagine a spouse being so intuitive they could read your body language all day long. Looking into his eyes, we see another being in there, which is what it feels like when I see the black wolf in the woods, a painting that sits in my office. An incredibly intelligent creature who just wants to help make our lives a better one.

Soon our daily routine consisted of Teddy going to the fence and leaning against it, to indicate he wanted to visit the neighbors. I would get a text saying, "Teddy is by the fence" or a picture of him as a way of communicating those words. I would go outside and hand him over, chit-chat a little with Ghaida, the woman of the house, and return inside. Sometimes our chats led to a tiny smoke in the kitchen, and as a result, my delicious world famous *"well* done" beef tikka, although my husband had a difference in opinion. Her and I talked about everything —my mother's death, her mother's death, our children, our problems. Later in the day Teddy would either come to the end of their fence and we'd see him from our window, or we'd get a text saying, "Teddy wants to leave." If it was late at night, we'd text the neighbors, asking, "Teddy ready to come home?"

On a few occasions the backyard was so wet or slippery that we drove him back and forth as one would their child. Often during our daily walks, Teddy would stop at their house which was on our route home. They would open the door, I would hand over the leash, and he would go inside where a lunch of chicken awaited him.

Teddy brought as much joy and healing to the neighbors as he did for us. During the pandemic, Ghaida's father ended up in the hospital for weeks and she kept Teddy at her house longer than usual as he comforted her. Whenever someone passed away, especially a dog, Teddy knew, he just knew, and he treated the mourner differently, staring into their eyes lovingly, sadly, as if to say, "I understand, and it'll be okay." Even if the person was a stranger, Teddy sensed their loss. It felt as if he also sensed the auras and spirits of the deceased. He was a mediator between joy and sorrow.

The kids loved him too. When I dropped off my son at elementary school, the children would gather around and fuss over him as he lay on the ground. He carried himself with so much pride and confidence, walking around thinking he's a big shot, that kids started calling him "Trump." When he got close to them, he laid down and stayed put as he patiently allowed them to pet him. "He's so soft!" they cried. "He's so cute!"

I sighed, leaving the world behind and staring into the fire, remembering how once upon a time, my mother sat in her wheelchair just a few feet away, where Teddy was now lying on his blue, cozy bed with a red blanket as a pillow. While I listened in my office to classical or shamanic music, Indian or Latin songs, Mom would watch the Arabic movie channel, which played reruns of old classics with legendary actors like Omar Sharif, Faten Hamama, Rushdy Abaza, Mervat Amin, and the list goes on. Most of them have passed away, except for Adel Emam and a few others. I loved those films. They were rich in story, good acting, and high-quality production. They didn't have the basic cheap formula that movies of later times had in order to make a quick buck. The opening overtures of those classic films are still unmatched.

Occasionally I had the news on when something exciting was happening. I would talk with her and get her engaged, asking, "Mom, what do you think about our new president?"

"What's his name?" she asked, interested.

"Trump."

She nodded assuredly. "He speaks quite lovely."

I laughed, since she knew few words in English, or that's what she always claimed anyway. The presence of my mom, and those classic Arabic films, embedded my heart and soul with the sense of warmth that belonged to the olden days. The atmosphere also influenced the rhythm of my writing, helping me surrender into the act like one surrenders into a dance, a meditation, a succulent meal. I loved our mornings together. They were heavenly. Then one day they were gone, and ever since, I haven't been able to watch those Arabic movies.

A ping from my phone brought me back to the room. "Can we have Teddy please?"

The snow was a couple of inches high, but I put on my sandals that awaited me by the sliding door next to a towel to keep the floor dry from all the in-and-out foot and paw traffic. Teddy stood beside me wiggling his tail, excitedly awaiting the visit, even though it was not the first or second one of that day. I picked him up to ensure he didn't run outside and make us chase him through the cold snow as he tended to do when he was in the mood to play, causing us to beg and negotiate and try to trick him to no avail. He would end up hiding under the trampoline with us cussing beneath our breath as we went back inside the house, unable to endure the harsh cold that this little wolf absolutely loved.

I took short steps over the slippery spots toward the fence. The neighbor awaited me, a blanket wrapped around her. She too had sandals on but at least she wore socks. Over the years, I'd seen her come out with bath towels, lingerie, pajamas, evening dresses, or whatever other clothes items she was in, to get Teddy. I passed Teddy to her blanketed arms. She baby talked to him, with her higher pitched and sing-songy voice that always accompanied her warm embrace. We then each returned inside our homes, both feeling full by his boundless love, by the doll we shared that has brought forth the child within us.

CHAPTER 10

THE BACKYARD WEDDING

As my husband drove us to my very first at-home wedding, a backyard wedding, I felt excited to experience something new. Through the car window I watched the small towns and rural areas we passed by, and I recalled the wedding of Thomas Edison's oldest and most favorite sister, Marion. Of course, I did not attend Marion's wedding in person. It was in 1849, more than a hundred years before my birth—not that I would have been invited if I had already been birthed. But when the lovely and well-spoken tour guide lady at Thomas Edison's small brick Greek revival home-turned-museum showed us the parlor where Marion wed, she helped magically transport me to that Victorian Era. I imagined Marion wearing a white wedding dress, popularized by Queen Victoria in 1840. The queen wore a white dress of Spitafields silk and Honiton lace to her wedding, breaking from custom and initiating a lasting tradition for Western bridal fashion. Prior, brides had the choice to wear any color they desired, including black. Sometimes they even wore patterns such as stripes, plaids, checks, or paisleys. White was considered an impractical color.

After the nuptials, Marion's small guest party must have enjoyed a grand buffet or a spectacular catered dinner, or perhaps it was a potluck in the little garden, although wait a minute… her wedding took place in the winter and in December the weather in Ohio is cold, maybe rainy or snowy. The house sat on the hill above the old Milan Canal, so the weather was probably even worse. No, the dinner reception couldn't have been outdoors. It must have been an intimate affair, as most weddings were of that era, with only immediate relatives attending the ceremony, and most likely it didn't include a lavish dinner or other delicacies.

We arrived, I finally realized, noticing my husband slowing down and navigating through a busy area. Cars parked over the lawn, in front of the house, and across the street. An old 1950's Chevy was sitting on the lawn in front of the two-story house. I gathered my purse and switched eras, slipping out of Marion's December 1849 wedding to attend the July 2017 wedding.

"I'm overdressed," I said, looking at the people standing outside, dressed in shorts and jeans. "Why didn't you tell me what they would be wearing?"

"I told you the groom will be wearing cowboy jeans."

"You never said that." This responsibility fell on his shoulders since the bride, a longtime employee of his, had invited him.

I stepped out in my A-line polka dot dress that flared beneath the knees. My long necklace with heart-shaped pendant dangled between my breasts. My long hair flowed around me, and it just so happened that I'd worn my diamond wedding ring—something I rarely did these days even on special occasions. My husband had on nice dress pants and a dress shirt. I felt the eyes of the guests burning into our backs as we passed them, while those in front of us gingerly smiled and nodded. I wondered if there was an etiquette for being overdressed, that perhaps we should apologize to the hostess or something, and explain that we are, after all, Chaldean.

Modern Chaldean weddings in the U.S. are filled with glitz and glam, with couples spending an obscene amount of money to impress their guests. The typical wedding day starts at the bride's house. While the groom is at the church with his groomsmen, his family heads over to the bride's house in a large singing and dancing procession where the bride gives corsages to the family and takes photos with them. The groom does something similar when preparing at his own house. On occasion, a male relative of the bride will follow the old village custom and close the doors of her home, otherwise known as the blocking-of-the-doorway, refusing to let the bride leave without receiving payment from the groom's family. An amount is requested and must be met before the bride can leave for the church. In the villages of Iraq, people often offered a box of live chicken or *Arak*, an alcoholic drink, as payment. In the States, however, a flock of poultry did not make a useful bridal gift, no matter how many fresh eggs they could produce. Back home, the tradition was also more light-hearted and playful whereas in the U.S. some people treated it like a business transaction. A few weddings were nearly called off due to either the groom's side being offended by the im-pudence of the request, or the bride's side being insulted by the inadequate response.

My husband, Sudaid, and I walked over the grass onto the driveway. A young woman in a simple burgundy dress greeted us. "I had on something nicer earlier, but I changed because Brian smeared cake on me and it fell on my clothes and went into my nose."

I realized this was the bride. Kissing her on both cheeks, I blessed and congratulated her. She invited us into the garage where long tables of food were set up and she told us to eat. Her father had catered food from Kroger and the salesmen at my husband's store gifted her the beer and liquor. Sudaid said he'd wait a little before eating, but I was hungry and piled sal-ads on a plate and made a drink. We walked to a white canopy tent set up with garden tables and chairs and sat down. The people chatted at the table beside us as country music played in the background. It was beautiful and quite different from what we were accustomed to.

For decades, Chaldean American receptions have been held at either Penna's (for East Siders) in Sterling Heights or Shenandoah (for West Siders) in West Bloomfield, because, well, where else would one have it? The *zaffa*, the grand entrance when the couple enter the reception, starts with Middle Eastern music and people cheering. The celebratory wedding march is a musical procession of drums, horns, and pipes. Sometimes belly dancers and men would carry flaming swords or the bride on a palanquin, an enclosed bed mounted on poles carried at each end on men's shoulders. Anthropologists don't know exactly when this timeless tradition started, but most believe it originated in ancient Egypt. Palanquins were used in ancient times by Indian, Chinese, Persian and Roman royalty, or people of great importance for long trips. They were often large enough for sleeping and dining in. When the wedding procession reaches its destination, the family and friends of the newly married couple join in the festivities, dancing, and merry making.

A Chaldean American reception is an explosion of color, music, and love, styled from head to toe with bursts of rich flowers, chandeliers of grand proportions, magnificent dresses, tables of desert, and countless other gorgeous decors. It's the ultimate over-the-top celebration. But sometimes it's a bit too much, like when the flower centerpieces are as large as a miniature tree and therefore you must bend sideways to a ninety-degree position to speak to the person on the other side of the table. Or when the bride's competitiveness causes her to buy the biggest fairytale dress imaginable, in her opinion anyway, which stuns the guests in the opposite direction. They end up describing it as a "Halloween costume."

For the most part, you don't have variety between the ten to twenty weddings you're invited to per year. It would be more exciting and would feel less of an obligation to, for instance, attend a wedding at the Detroit Yacht Club one day, another day at the Scarab Club or the Dearborn Inn, and another day in the groom's backyard. One day we attend a wedding of over a thousand guests, another day two hundred guests, and maybe another day, a wedding of around thirty guests, which is not very probable but not impossible.

The taco salad was tasty, and I ate quite a bit of it. I felt comfortable, though I knew I was sticking out like a deer in an empty pasture and people continued to stare. I shared my feelings with my husband and he said with his assuring and confident smile, "I like it here. I like the atmosphere. You look nice dressed like that with your husband."

I looked around. "How many acres of land do you think this is?"

"A lot," he said. "They are wealthy countryfolks. They just live a simple lifestyle."

It did feel nice to break free from the routine, the countless fancy-dressed glamour girls showing their curves, cleavage and gold, and dancing in the middle of the extravagant dance floor. The single men spending the night at the bar, gawking at potential brides of their own. The super loud music, thanks to the band's sound system meant for concerts, that left you with headaches, ringing ears, and possible irreversible ear damage or a sore throat for having to scream at the person beside you. The late night four course meal of soup, salad, an entrée of steak, chicken, potatoes and green beans, followed by ice cream and cake with coffee. In the case of Penna's, you get full early on their famous hot and delicious cream of broccoli soup and their Italian herb bread. Tony, the owner of Penna's, promises his guests a free tub of cream of broccoli soup. All you have to do is drive to the back of the building after the party is over and request it from the kitchen staff. The next day, whoever goes through the trouble to get the tub would pass soup in smaller containers to their relatives, while it was still fresh, like one would share their surplus of garden fruits and vegetables.

Penna's felt like a second home to Chaldean East Siders, to the point where we thought we knew everything about this luxury authentic Italian banquet hall. The ceiling tiles and chandeliers are from the 1900's. Parties are executed to a science, except when staff cleans up so fast, we don't get a chance to enjoy the appetizers or desserts. Then one day, my son asked, "Mom, did you know that Penna's is actually Penna apostrophe 's'?"

"What?" I asked, confused.

"You know how Chaldeans pronounce it Pennas? But it's Penna, then apostrophe 's'."

Although the apostrophe had always been there on the sign, the wrong pronunciation led Chaldeans to believe that Pennas, not Penna, was the owner's last name.

After a while Sudaid made himself a plate of food. We ate quietly and with joy, entering a dreamlike succulent state. The atmosphere was simple but exquisite. The intimacy of it felt warm and sweet, filled with the lovely little touches that resemble the frothy hearts in a café latté. It reminded me of the Chaldean weddings of the past, particularly the ones that took place in the village "back home." I never attended one there but I heard plenty of stories, and Dr. Adhid Miri describes it in detail in the article "Traditional Chaldean Weddings" published by *The Chaldean News.*

The villagers had open-air weddings, where all the neighbors and strangers—though there were no strangers at that time—could join in. A jester would go into the center of town and call out loudly, without a microphone, the invitation for the wedding, adding, "Everyone invited and not invited, join us!"

On the wedding day, the groom, his parents, and his relatives would walk to the bride's home in the big procession. Women followed the men as they sang folksongs and did *hallahil*, ululations, while a traditional folklore band played the *zarna* and *tabul*, a double reed wind instrument and a brass drum. The bride appeared in her white dress and began to walk in front of the ladies. Everyone then headed to the church for the ceremony, and afterward, the procession would continue as people headed to the reception at the groom's house. They stopped at every corner to sing, drink, and dance. Neighbors stood at their doors, celebrating along by presenting trays of sweets, pitchers of water, and a bottle of Arak with glass cups for shots. The mirth would pause near homes that had experienced a recent calamity or the death of a loved one.

The bride would be paraded around the village riding an adorned horse, which Dr. Miri calls "the limo of those days." A child sat in front of her and another behind her and her gifts and *jihaz*, wedding accessories, were mounted on a second horse. The wedding celebrations lasted four days, and on the last night, the hosts would serve their guests a large pot of *piqoota* (barley) and chicken. This meal indicated for everyone that the party was over, it's time to go home. The guests obliged, and before leaving, sang the last Aramaic chant, "Fill and fill our bottles and cups…today we drink, tomorrow you kick us out."

The scene resembled the one of Michael Corleone and Appolonia's Sicilian wedding in the first *Godfather* movie. The open invitations stopped, for various purposes, and over time, people started having their weddings inside banquet halls in Mosul. Some say that couples began following the western wedding styles. Others say that when the population of non-Christians increased in the village, the male strangers who attended the weddings and took their shots of Arak would then pester the girls, since to some, Christian girls were considered fair game.

A Boxer Pit Bull came running beside us. Sudaid asked the bride's mother sitting across from us if we could feed him. "Yes," she said. "As long as there's no bones. You can give him the fat."

Before we could offer him food, the Pit Bull ran in a different direction. He went to the volleyball net where two young girls my preteen daughter's age were playing. We laughed at this bundle of cuteness. Then Sudaid asked if I wanted to take a walk by the water while he smoked. I said yes and followed him. We watched a little stream of water near the fence.

"She says fish come through here," he said. He loved watching fish swim down the stream. It reminded him of when his father took him and his siblings on fishing trips in Iraq.

We walked further down and saw chairs around a fire pit with no fire, only smoke caused by burnt grass clippings.

"It smells strange," I said.

"Because the grass is wet," my husband said.

I imagined us grabbing a nice sized blanket to sit on in front of the stream, away from the stress of the narrow world beaten by a heavy amount of overbearing political and religious views. Here, we could relax, calm our minds, and enjoy a broader and deeper view of the world. We could blend with the sensations that we had before we were born, when we were cushioned by the waters of water, the womb. Nature is the real science of the universe.

We returned to the party where the bride joined the girls in playing volleyball. The Pit Bull made us laugh as he jumped for the ball. At one point, he ran off with it in his teeth. Everyone chased him to grab hold of the ball before he popped it. We all laughed wholeheartedly. Sudaid and I walked to the old Chevy parked right on the front yard. He noticed the new license plate and said that the car was drivable. The interior was all messed up, with cotton pulled out of the cushions and dust everywhere. A sign in the back seat read "Moonshine Merchandise for Sale."

We headed toward a man, who I later learned was the bride's father, to ask him about the car. He didn't know the car's production year and instead ended up telling us about a man he grew up with who was now some eighty-seven years old, a Tom Holden. "He's like five feet tall, has strands of hair up to his waist that he puts in a ponytail, small eyes like Chinese, and has trophies you can see from the window which have tons of dust. He's the owner of Kustoms Unlimited auto shop and has painted and done the cars of famous celebrities like Tom Selleck."

He told us about the sign in front of Holden's house with the number ninety-three, "or something like that," and beside it, it says, "'We're now calling number seven' or something like that." He laughed. "He's just a smart aleck. When he walks around, you'd never guess he'd won all those trophies. He could care less about that. Now he doesn't work anymore, but his son is doing the work just like him if not better."

I listened, intrigued, and wanting to vanish into simpler days when I was less ambitious, a bit oblivious, and didn't rely so much on the clock. When apple and blackberry were just fruits, and television noise didn't pierce the ears like a sewing needle. My idea of simplicity didn't mean living in a cabin, baking bread from scratch, chopping my own wood, fishing, and chasing bears away. It meant building it the way I wanted it to be; a quaint home in a small community with nice neighbors and little noise, great food, a cozy place for writing, reading, and even resting, and lots of space to focus. *Wait a minute… I* thought, considering my current lifestyle.

Sudaid told the bride's father that I loved history, adding, "She's a writer."

"You're a writer?" the man said. "Then look into Lake Superior and how it eats things right up. Have you heard of the SS Edmund Fitzgerald?"

"Yes," I responded, having only heard of it and nothing else.

"It sunk in Lake Superior in 1975, killing all twenty-nine crew members on board. Nature can kill you. Yes, it's beautiful when the flowers and the sun are out, but it can kill you just like that!" He snapped his fingers.

Launched in 1958 as the biggest carrier in the Great Lakes, the man explained, the ship became the first to carry more than a million tons of iron through the Soo Locks. On November 10, 1975, a severe winter storm developed with ten-feet-high waves and winds of sixty miles per hour. The vessel sank and no bodies were ever recovered from the wreckage. Later, the ship was discovered broken into two, approximately 150 feet apart. It still sits 530 feet deep, at the bottom of Lake Superior.

We left the wedding shortly after dark. On our way home, I searched Google for Tom Holden's shop. The address came up on the map, absent of a website, social media handles, and whatever other hype businesses used to publicize their products and services. The shop evidently relied on quality workmanship, probably not so much on customer service. I looked out the window to get a glimpse of the shop and as we passed by, I could barely see anything through the window in the dark, let alone that sign that said, "You're seventh in the line of ninety-three-something."

Five years passed when I came across the journal entry of July 23, 2017 of the backyard wedding. I researched Kustoms Unlimited online to find the address and plan a visit. I was surprised to find his obituary. Thomas A. Holden passed away two years ago at age ninety-one. He started his business in 1951. He had a love for mechanics and flight and had built many gas-powered model airplanes, mostly of his own design. After graduating Roseville High School in 1947, he joined the United States Air Force, serving for twenty years before retiring at the rank of Master Sergeant. Some of his crowning achievements included a long list of awards. Tom always knew what he wanted and would say, "When I go, I don't want anyone fussing, sending flowers or the rest of the 'pazazz and razza mataz'… From the gurney to the fireplace. Then if you want, set up a keg of Budweiser and/or Verners in the middle of the shop and have a party with anyone that wants to come."

I closed my journal and stared at its cover, a painting of *Bridge over a Pond of Water Lilies* by Claude Monet. The stories written on its pages belonged largely to the year 2017, when my mother was still alive. Holden's attitude reminded me of hers. She knew who she was and what she wanted. She acted with precision and confidence, and repeated time and time again that she did not want us to wear black for any mourning period after she passed away. Of course, she aimed the message at her daughters. Men didn't have to follow this tradition, although usually they were to remain unkempt and not shave for forty days. Typically, the period to wear black was forty days for the more distant mourners, such as cousins or nieces, and for the closer mourners, such as daughters, up to one year. During this time, they also do not dance or celebrate any major events. Afterward, they begin wearing brightly colored clothes signifying the end of the mourning period and the idea that life must continue.

The tradition of wearing black dates to the Roman Empire when the family of the deceased would wear a dark-colored *toga*, called a *toga pulla*. The tradition persisted in England throughout medieval times, when women were expected to wear black caps and veils when their husbands passed away. The color black is not based on any text in Arab countries, including the religion of Islam. The custom gained popularity as funeral fashion after the death of Prince Albert in 1861, when Queen Victoria wore black until she died forty years later to show she was a grieving widow.

Despite my mother's wishes, we did wear black for about six months and took it off in time for one of my niece's weddings. She, like several of my nieces, married a non-Chaldean man, so the wedding had a little over three hundred guests and was less over-the-top. It reminded me of weddings a few decades ago, when the bride and groom headed the reception line. Over time, the two sets of parents from both sides replaced them. Since a wedding day flew by as quickly as a flock of birds, it became impossible for even the parents of the bride and groom to guarantee that single meaningful moment with each of the five-hundred-plus guests. So, the reception line was eliminated altogether.

Due to the pressures of planning a luxury wedding, some couples end up calling off their engagement. Many put themselves in debt. Even though money is traditionally given to the bride and groom because it's understood to be more useful than gifts, couples are lucky to walk away breaking even with such high wedding costs.

Still, at the end of the day, Chaldean weddings are full of fun, love, and radiance. For us, large celebrations are a way to honor life, the Creator, and our ancestors, who stem from an empire widely known for its fantastic, oversized buildings, such as the Ishtar Gate and the Hanging Gardens, one of the Seven Wonders of the World. The Ishtar Gate was nearly fifty feet high, a hundred feet wide, made of blue glazed bricks and decorated with bas-relief dragons and young bulls and lions. King Nebuchadnezzar II, who ruled Babylon from 605 BC for forty-three years, is said to have had the Hanging Gardens built to be about seventy-five feet high. If the gardens existed, it would have taken 8,200 gallons of water each day to keep the plants watered. Being over-the-top is in our blood.

CHAPTER 11

CHALDEAN MEN

Dressed in black, my sisters and I stood in front of the fancy door that belonged to Cousin Helene's large home on Tuscany Drive. The Tuscany in Sterling Heights, which is barely three decades old and is of close driving distance from home, is different than the Tuscany in Italy. The original Tuscany, which requires a lengthy trip via airplane to reach, derives its name from the Etruscan tribe which settled there about 1000 BC. The Italian Tuscany is known for its landscapes, history, artistic legacy, and its influence on high culture, whereas the American Tuscany suburb isn't well known at all, and about all you'll see there are deer, squirrels, birds, kids playing in the yard, and people jogging or walking their dogs.

Aunt Ameera accompanied us, holding a large Iraqi orange cake she was famous for baking. Its distinctive smell touched our pallets as we waited for the door to open. There's a custom after someone dies that you visit the family's home, even though you already paid your respects by going to the funeral. This applies mostly to the closer relatives, and although it's not done as often as in the olden days, it's still practiced. One of Helene's brothers, Khairy, had died earlier in the year of leukemia, so here we were, practicing a custom which in my earlier years I was excluded from. But now I was officially a grown-up woman who had to perform certain duties.

I closed my mind and listened to the evening hour. The season neared the end of winter, and the trees and flowers were asleep, awaiting spring. The door opened and we entered the spacious house that resembled where I lived before I got married, the big, beautiful house that overlooked a pond. I lived there with my mother, my brother, and his wife and two children. Now my brother and his wife have three children and they live in a pleasant but less lavish house across the street from my own. We watch each other's homes without being intrusive, and when needed, we asked for potatoes, onions, eggs, tomatoes, saffron, turmeric, milk, or more important things like picking up or dropping off each other's children at school.

In traditional Middle Eastern societies, it's customary for couples to start out their marriage living with the husband's family while they build a house or save money. This living arrangement is diminishing at a very fast rate in the Arab world and is almost nonexistent in the Western world, although once upon a time, it did exist in the West.

At Helene's house, two other women were present, related through marriage. The nine of us sat around the kitchen table, looking like crows. A late evening brunch was spread on the kitchen island. It consisted of the cake my aunt brought, pasties, homemade pizza, pickled vegetables, parsley, chives, fresh vegetables, and other delicacies. Tea was served. We ate and brought up several topics, starting with a popular Chaldean priest who had offended some of the women at the table. Their main grudge was that he threw offensive remarks around as if he were playing a game of darts. Anyone who stepped outside the norm or bathed in lavish lifestyles was a legit target.

"The moment he condemned anyone who buys Gucci and Versace purses, I picked up my Luis Vuitton handbag and walked out of the church," one chic woman said, straightening herself.

The subject then turned to men. One of the women, the only widow at the table, was married to our cousin, Latif, who was known for his bad temper when he was single even though his name meant "nice." People said, "God help the woman who marries him." But after he got married, he changed. He softened. He became the ideal husband and helped his wife in many ways. "She controlled him," Helene said, and we all laughed, including the widow.

Helene, the only sister to seven brothers, served her brothers day and night. Some were picky eaters and expected their food to be prepared quite particularly, served with a certain garnish and such. One brother was so needy, he expected *everything* to be done for him. "We'd hang his underpants out to dry, and when he came home, he expected us to place one leg in each opening," she said, most seriously.

We laughed so hard that tears came down our eyes.

"Then after he got married," she continued, "he began to cook all the complicated Iraqi dishes reserved for women because his wife did not know how to cook. He cooked for himself and oftentimes the family. Many of my other brothers who were picky eaters ended up doing the same."

"I support men helping out their wives, especially nowadays," said the widow. "Women are also bringing home income and she shouldn't have to do all the household duties and take care of the kids on her own."

"Each man is different," Helene said. "Many change drastically after they get married, and some continue to be waited on hand and foot. It depends on the man. My husband, for instance, will turn off the car, get out, and head to the door leaving the groceries in the trunk. I call after him, 'I need help! Help me! Help me!'" She demonstrated by folding her body over the table and stretching her arms in desperation. "But by then, he's inside and the door is closed."

We laughed hysterically as she continued, "He says, 'Helene, you don't have to do anything, don't bother with this or that.' I tell him, 'I need to clean the house.' He says, 'You don't have to.' I tell him, 'I have to cook.' He says, 'You don't have to.'"

"Then how does he think things will get done?" my sister asked.

She shrugged. "That's the thing!"

The woman who walked out of the church because of the priest's anti-brand-name purse remarks, re-told a story that happened over forty years ago. She had invited my oldest brother and his wife over for *pacha*, a traditional Iraqi stew made from sheep's head, trotters, and stomach; sheep brain, cheeks, tongues, are sometimes included—even eyeballs, though many people prefer to remove them before cooking. For Chaldeans, Easter and Christmas dinner is not complete without pacha. The time, work, and cost involved makes it reserved for holidays and special occasions. The woman placed the pacha in the oven without water. Hours later smoke filled the house. The guests arrived to a burnt dinner.

I loved these women. Most of them had gotten married the old-fashioned way, being courted for a short time before accepting a formal wedding proposal in the presence of family. Their relationships snowballed into a love, respect, admiration, trust and reliance, the likes which seems impossible in our modern American society. The men adored their wives beyond measure. Back then, people had responsibilities to each other. Today, they turn their dreams of marriage into a nightmare.

With the exception of the widow, these women were in my life before I was born. For instance, Helene's mother, Hania was first to hold me the day of my birth. Story has it that my mother's water broke while she was in the shower. She told my fifteen-year-old sister Niran to call the midwife. Naturally, we didn't have a phone. Therefore, Niran went to a neighbor who had one. The midwife wasn't home, so Niran left a message with a family member and returned to my mother with the bad news. My mother told her to try again. On the way to the neighbor's Niran saw my great-uncle's wife, Hania, approaching with one of her seven sons.

"I noticed your mother hasn't visited anyone for the past three days," Aunt Hania said. "Something told me to check up on her."

Since a phone call wasn't an option, and letters were too formal and took a long time to deliver, and most were illiterate to read or write them, people communicated through the cheapest, most accurate method—their senses. Aunt Hassina had a feeling that something was happening, and she was right on.

Niran related to Aunt Hania the desperate situation she was in. Aunt Hania didn't even blink an eye. Marching inside our home, she removed her *abaya*, a long black cloak that, back then, covered the body but not necessarily the hair, worn mostly for convenience. She did so in a swift and stoic manner, to show the seriousness of the matter at hand and the professional substitute she would be for the task. "No need to get the midwife," she said. "I'll deliver the baby myself. Just bring hot water and rags."

Niran rushed to the kitchen and my great aunt went to my mother's side. As Aunt Hania ushered me out of my mother's womb, she repeatedly told my mother not to worry, not to be afraid. She also said to my mom, "If it's a boy, you can keep him. If it's a girl, I'll take her for my youngest son."

She meant when I grew up. Her son needed to grow up too. At that time, he was still in diapers. And when he did grow up, he married a Greek woman and they had beautiful children. Then he died in his forties of a heart attack.

The midwife arrived in time to cut the cord, which wasn't long afterward. I was an easy birth. My mother was in labor hardly an hour before I came out. I was named Weam by I don't know who, although I grew up thinking my sister Nidhal named me. Weam is a unisex name and it means harmony, peace and love, particularly between friends or nations.

At the kitchen table, Niran reminded us of the day when Latif was brought to our house in Baghdad by two men holding him from each arm. He had injured his leg and came to see my father. My father, Hermiz, was the head of the accounting department at Baghdad's railroad station. For additional income, he translated and interpreted Arabic to English and English to Arabic. For no charge, he tutored students. Friends sent their high school children who would sit in the living room waiting his arrival. He could tackle any subject; math, English, physics. He also went to court as a counsel for those who couldn't afford attorneys and didn't have the language sophistication, or basic smarts, to defend themselves. Once his nephew was accused of theft by his employer. My father went through the accounts so diligently that he discovered the mathematical mistake that led to the accusation and proved his nephew's innocence.

He was also a medicine man, a bonesetter. People with broken bones or sprained muscles or ligaments came to him rather than going to a doctor or the hospital. As soon as the patient arrived, my mother would fill warm water into the wide round tub she used to wash laundry. She would bring the tub to the living room along with towels and a big hard green bar of handmade soap. The soap, made mostly of olive oil, is what everyone in Iraq used to wash their hands, body, and hair. It was brown on the outside because of oxidation and green inside, had a pleasant smokey scent, was creamy instead of lathery, and was a good cleanser and moisturizer for the hair and skin; it even helped remove acne. It seems that its recipe has remained unchanged for more than two thousand years.

We watched grown men cry and scream in pain as he rubbed the injured area with the soap that evidently had some therapeutic effects. References to soap have been found in ancient Iraq's Sumerian tablets dating back four thousand years, when soap paste, made from ash and vegetable fats, was used to treat wounds and skin disorders. Babylonians were making soap consisting of water, alkali and cassia oil as early as 2800 BC for washing and medical purposes.

The widow said that my dad had also healed her one-year-old son here in America. They had left him with a relative and when they came home, they noticed the baby wouldn't stop crying. The mother asked the babysitter what had happened. The babysitter explained that when she went to pick him up, she'd pulled him from the arm and noticed afterward he wouldn't stop crying. Latif called on my dad right away. They bundled the baby and rushed to our home. The whole ritual of the water and olive oil appeared before her eyes. Within minutes, my father pulled the baby's arm, something clicked, and the baby stopped crying. All was good.

The baby had moved so much that water spilled from the tub onto my father's pajamas, so Latif told his wife. "Buy him two new pajamas tomorrow!" which she did.

My sisters and I had never heard this story before.

We went on to share other memories. Helene said that after she wed, her mother Hania called her every morning at 7:30 a.m. to pray for fifteen minutes, something they did together before she left her home. Helene told her mother that particular hour was awfully early, and her mother would say, "It's what we did every day before."

"Yes, *youm*, but now I'm married and well...." Helene stopped short of explaining that she... well, had other personal duties to perform that early in the morning.

"We must do this first thing in the morning. Otherwise, you'll start doing other things, get too busy, and forget."

Aunt Hassina buried twin daughters, Helene's would-be-sisters. They died on April 1, 1949, when a massive flood drowned forty-four people in Tel Keppe. Forty-two of them were young girls at a school. One of them was an eighteenth-month-old baby and the other, a grown man. Survivors remember the sky turning dark and raindrops the size of golf balls falling hard. The town was angry at the teacher who, for some reason, did not allow the girls to leave the classroom. She survived and the townspeople wanted her charged for murder, even hung, neither of which happened.

The evening was done and we all went our separate ways, only for the sisters to later call each other to share notes about some petty, and somewhat comical drama that had taken place between two of the women. The following night I drove to my sister Niran's house with Teddy. The garbage men had arrived at our home earlier than usual, around 7:30 a.m., and so I was stuck with three bags of garbage. Thank goodness I had sisters who lived nearby with different garbage pickup dates.

My sister and I drank tea and ate from a plate of walnuts, dates, cashews, pistachios, and almonds as she shared stories I'd never heard about my dad—his simple, kind, and genius ways. Her husband, who has muscular dystrophy and is bound to a hospital bed, sat on the far-right corner watching a black and white Egyptian film, a classic. He asked me if I knew where I could find a book about Al Mutanabbi in Arabic.

"Do you know Al Mutanabbi?" he asked.

"Isn't that a street in Baghdad?" I asked.

"He was a famous Arab poet."

"Najah, you already have that book!" my sister said.

"Weam, do you know where I can find it?" he asked me, avoiding her remark.

She looked at me. "He has it."

I promised I would get him that book before I walked out of the house, curious about this poet's name, one I had only ever known as a street name. Al Mutanabbi was a historic center of Baghdad books, filled with bookstores and outdoor book stalls. It was referred to as the heart and soul of Baghdad literacy and intellectual community. A suicide bomb exploded there on March 5, 2007, and killed twenty-six people, leaving the area littered and unsafe for shops, destroying many businesses. Today, the rubble has been cleared and the road is recovering. But many Iraqi writers live in exile because of ongoing sectarian violence.

That night, I thought about my dad and his progressive ways. He had paid for his sister, my Aunt Hassina, to go to nursing school. She ended up becoming the midwife of Fallujah. People were constantly knocking on her door in the middle of the night. "Um Sabri, Um Sabri! So and so is in labor!" She would stumble out of bed, put on her *abbaya*, and run outside. The next day you'd see servants or country people approach her home with boxes of live chickens, fresh eggs, dried dates, and figs. That's how she was repaid, and of course, with money too.

Mostly Aunt Hassina delivered babies of the wives and daughters of sheiks. She worked for decades amongst tribes who universally loved and respected her. She also helped save a number of lives, especially newborn girls. Long ago, when Fallujah was just a small town, it was customary amongst Arab tribes for the father, if he so desired, to bury a newborn girl. Some men wanted to do just that, and my aunt was such an educated, smart, and compassionate woman that she was able to convince them not to.

"How did she do that?" I once asked another aunt

during my visit to Iraq. She and I were on a bus heading from Baghdad to Tel Keppe.

"With an effective tongue, how else?"

"I mean, what did she say to them?" I asked.

"She used anecdotes from their Quran, because, you see, Islam forbids such evil acts," she said in a whisper, as she lightly tapped the one free hand she had over my hand. "In the Quran, it is said that on Judgment Day, buried girls will rise out of their graves and ask for what crime they were killed."

Fallujah, which dates back to Babylonian times, was host to important Jewish academies for centuries and later became known as the city of mosques because of its over two hundred mosques. During the Gulf War, Fallujah suffered one of the highest tolls of civilian casualties. Two separate failed bombing attempts on Fallujah's bridge over the Euphrates River hit crowded markets, killing an estimated six hundred civilians. Aunt Hassina was not around during the war. She had died in the 1980s.

My father's progressiveness, of course, influenced his daughters as well as my four brothers. When he passed away, I was only fifteen years old, and my three older brothers then took on the role of my father. They did not put the kind of restrictions on me that my Chaldean friends' brothers put on them. They protected me and made sure I had what I needed to have a good life without holding me back from anything or hurrying me off to get married. Not prohibited from having different experiences, I didn't feel that I had to go get something that was not mine. That gave me a sense of self-respect and freedom, the will to choose, rather than to grab or resist something merely because it is "forbidden."

And while they may or may not do the cooking and

laundry and other household tasks for their wives, they have encouraged their daughters to fly and taught their sons to be loving, respectful men. Their loyalty to their people and devotion to their community doesn't interfere with their humble, open-minded ways that puts people at ease. I am grateful to say the Chaldean men I grew up with are good men.

Part III

THE FUTURE

CHAPTER 12

THE WORLD'S FIRST AND ONLY CHALDEAN MUSEUM

It was a gloomy cold day in May. Driving to the museum, I passed the cemetery where my mother lay, the headstone not yet having been installed, the ground fresh with snow and rain, the groundskeeper waiting for the grass to grow. Her burial lot was near the main road, a fence separating her from the traffic. Additional separation was, of course, the fact that she was among the dead while I was among the living, in the physical sense at least. If we were to measure spirits with a measuring cup or a spoon, we may find the opposite is true. We may be dead compared to the dead. Whoever was alive or dead, whether the dead more alive than the living or the living more dead than the dead, since her burial, I could not find the circuit to truly connect with her.

I arrived at Shenandoah Country Club, a vast property with a golf course and the banquet hall for weddings that West Siders used so often, and I walked inside. To the right was the office and meeting room for the Chaldean Cultural Center, which houses the Chaldean Museum. I waited in the lobby until Judy, a middle-aged nice-looking brunette, showed up. I immediately felt comfortable by her down-to-earth mannerism and after we chitchatted briefly, she opened the entrance door to the museum.

Before I reached the threshold, the sound of a mysterious

foreign yet familiar music snuck through the doors like a streak of incense. Its pure and holy rhythm transported me to another world, one belonging to the ancients and the underground, where the spirits of my parents and ancestors greeted me, as if to say, "Welcome to our past." I entered the ancient gallery of the museum, imbued with the colors of copal blue, olive green, and gold that subtly represented that region and its surrounding Tigris and Euphrates Rivers. Judy explained that this was the Ancient Gallery, one of five of the museum's galleries. It focuses on the five main empires that ruled in ancient Mesopotamia: the Sumerian; the Akkadian; the Babylonian; the Assyrian; and the Neo-Babylonian (Chaldean).

The Ancient Gallery was a couple hundred feet, whereas the land it represented was about three hundred miles long and about fifteen hundred miles wide. We started with the Sumerians, and I was immediately transported to the stories of the people and places I've been reading about for over a decade, my people, my birthland, which I had heavily researched when writing my thirteenth and most recent book, *Mesopotamian Goddesses: Unveiling Your Feminine Power.* The book was published just four months prior to my visit to the museum and a month prior to my mother's death.

From that point forward, most of what Judy said and what I heard were two different things. I began to float along spontaneous streams of consciousness, my mind randomly taking me to where it wanted to go. Words I'd read over in the past suddenly appeared, organized into a partly historical, partly personal description of the Sumerians, who around 3500 BC, moved to the land between the Tigris and Euphrates Rivers in southern Mesopotamia, now called Iraq. It's not certain where they came from, but most likely they were nomads traveling in small groups until they had eaten the food and hunted the animals in their area, then moved on. In those days, people had the freedom to roam, to walk wherever they wanted in any desert or mountain, or to swim in lakes or rivers, and to sleep on uncultivated natural land under the visibility of the stars with the sound of the wind and animals. They went fishing, hunted, picked food from plants and trees, and felt their bare feet against the earth.

In Mesopotamia, the Sumerians learned without any books or type of formal education, that by planting seeds and plowing their land, they were able to grow crops. They domesticated or tamed the animals to help them plow their lands. Once food was plentiful, they relaxed a bit and began to use their intelligence to develop a most sophisticated civilization, one which has influenced our lives to this day. They formed several city-states, and walls around each of them to protect their citizens from outside invaders.

"This is a ziggurat," said Judy about a miniature replica of the Ziggurat of Ur stored behind a plastic screen. The real ziggurat was a huge, stepped structure similar to pyramids, only rectangular in shape, with a shrine at the summit. The Mayan people of Central America built similar structures. "This was built as a holy site to honor various gods. The Mesopotamians believed it connected heaven and earth."

My mind kept going elsewhere, and I wanted to leave my guide and follow my mind to see where it would take me. Perhaps I would arrive at an interesting never-before seen territory. It wouldn't be inappropriate for me to leave her, would it, given I already knew a great deal about ziggurats. In the city of Ur, King Ur-Nammu built a ziggurat nearly a hundred feet tall in honor of the god Sin. This was around 2100 BC, but the city was buried underneath fifteen feet of mud and sand, and the site wasn't discovered until 1850 by British archaeologists. Sir Leonard Woolley made vast excavation and investigative efforts in the 1920s and 1930s that dealt with the ziggurats, thousands of artifacts and tablets, as well as temples and graves in Mesopotamia. In the 1980s, Saddam Hussein restored the frontage of the lower foundation of the ziggurat and its massive staircases.

"Farmland was usually outside the city walls," Judy said, "and people would seek protection within the walls of the city when under attack."

Around the Ziggurat was a mockup of the people that lived in the marshes, their homes made of reeds to form arches. Reed mats were tied to create the walls and lattice panels allowed in light and air. The people there lived in secluded villages surrounded by rivers and *mashoofs* (long and narrow canoes), their main use of transportation. Their floating communities still exist, resembling the city of Venice, only much more ancient. Today, the people that live in the marshes are called Marsh Arabs and they are theorized by some to be the descendants of ancient Sumerians. Like other minorities in Iraq, the Marsh Arab population keeps shrinking, along with their stories. It's estimated there were 500,000 Marsh Arabs in the 1950s which decreased to about 20,000 following the draining that Saddam ordered to punish them for their insurrection against his regime. Thousands fled to Iran and returned after the 2003 Iraq invasion, only to suffer a decade later by a water shortage.

I imagined this fabled place where the Tigris and Euphrates rivers meet, which the Bible traces as the Garden of Eden and scholars describe as the cradle of civilization. Some historians say that the Chaldeans are Sumerians, since the ancient City of Ur is a Sumerian City, formerly known as the Ur of the Chaldees, and named after the Chaldeans who settled there between 6200-6500 BC. The city is said to be the birthplace of Prophet Abraham who married Sarah before he emigrated from Ur to the land of Canaan to continue calling people to worship one God, since Sumerians were polytheistic, believing in many gods. When a city was conquered, the invaders would force the conquered people to accept their gods.

It was shortly after this, somewhere between the jewelry of Queen Puabi and the statue of King Gudea, that I decided to abandon the tour and join the ancients. I removed my shoes and walked barefoot on the warm soft sand toward the ziggurat that glistened under the sun. I saw a village from afar with reed homes, fishing boats, and farm plots. I recognized them as the Marsh People. A young woman appeared from the midst of the village and approached me. She wore an abaya and greeted me in Arabic, although I knew her language was much more ancient than that, most likely Sumerian, an extinct language that was replaced by Akkadian within a short period of time.

"Are you going to the ziggurat?" she asked.

"Yes."

"It's quite a walk, but still nearby," she said. "Your mother is waiting for you there."

Her words sent a chill from the soles of my feet up into my brain. I wanted to ask questions, but she stared at me with a knowingness that said no further words need to be spoken. She then tightened her cloak around her waist and went about her way. I stared at the colossal rectangular pyramidal structure and hesitated. How could I possibly find my mother in there? Will it be dark by the time I reach the ziggurat? Is it safe to go alone to such a foreign place? Despite my questions going unanswered, I continued ahead. The sand held me, hugging my bare feet as I listened to the Earth assuring me that I was actually going to a place very familiar to my soul where I will recognize everyone and they will recognize me.

I arrived to the ziggurat. It had four sides and three monumental staircases that led up to a gate at the first terrace level. Next, a single staircase rose to a second terrace that supported a platform on which a temple and the final and highest terrace stood. The lower portion was supported by the first terrace and had some 720,000 baked bricks. A sign read, "It's forbidden to pick up anything from the ground regardless of how simple it is."

I picked up a small rock and stared at it, wondering how old it was, whether its age was in the millions or billions of years. Holding the rock in my hands, I walked forward and looked around for a sign of life. I saw a woman sitting on a small pasture that resembled a green rug. Between her thighs was a large bowl. As I came closer, her image became clearer and clearer and I thought to myself, who is this woman? She looks familiar.

She raised her head and her gaze locked onto mine. It took a moment before I realized she was my mother. The realization shook my strength and made my heart race. I tried to access the memory of whether she was alive or dead. Was I dreaming or was her previous death a dream and this moment an actual reality? Logic soon abandoned me, and I embraced her presence as a reality. This made her happy, and she smiled in assurance.

I went and squatted in front of her, and I watched her hands sorting the large barley in the bowl. She had the face of her younger years, when she only wore mumus, before she ever started wearing pants. She had on her original wedding ring, which she'd lost long ago. It was eventually replaced with another ring, and that ring was now on my finger, alongside my wedding ring.

"*Sabah al kheir.*" I greeted her with the Arabic words I used every morning when I went into her room to get her up from bed.

"*Sabah al noor, hala b'gawagh,*" she responded, partly in Arabic, partly in Aramaic. "*Mewat bewatha akha?*"

"I don't know what I'm doing here, or how I got here," I said, observing the place.

"How could you not know?" she asked, continuing in Aramaic as she returned her gaze to sorting barley. A few seconds later, she added, "You've come to visit the past."

This made me smile, reminding me of my early twenties, when I caused her grief and agony because I began to travel on my own to Europe, and later to the Middle East, and then to other parts of the world. She couldn't understand why I'd want to leave my comfortable life to explore new places, cultures, languages, and people. I simply found it exciting to travel, where no two days were the same, and I could experience an unsurpassable sense of freedom. I learned a great deal about myself and grew as a person by discovering how resourceful I could be. Traveling helped me realize that there is no one way to live life and that people's world views don't necessarily resemble mine. Having time and space to let my mind wander and take stock led me to get in touch with myself and discover different notions and possibilities. The more I traveled the more I appreciated my life, the more I understood what my mother was trying to teach me, that there's no place like home.

In my early thirties, my attitude toward traveling changed. I started to view it as hard work and having seen so many different places over the decades, the fun was gone. The more I loved and appreciated my home and family, the less desire I had to leave them. Beautiful and lovely things happened every day in my own backyard, so why obsess over getting to a distant land to experience them? Yet, although I stopped traveling overseas, I never really stopped traveling. I continued to visit places in my neighborhood, many which went unnoticed by those who were and were not from that community. My journalism assignments led me to deeper explorations, where I ended up covering extraordinary people and events. In my early forties, I was introduced to shamanism and began to visit my ancestors on a soul level.

"Do you know that you died?" I asked.

"I'm not dead," she said with calm awareness and acceptance.

I recalled the three dreams I had where I discovered Mom was not dead. The last one, when I worried about updating the Social Security office that she wasn't dead, occurred a week prior.

"How long have you been here?" I asked, coming out of the dream and into the land of Ur.

"Where?"

"At the ziggurat?"

"I came just for you. You've been calling me to show up in your dreams, but each time I tried, your grief got in the way."

"I'm grieving for you," I said.

"Put your grief aside, *brati*," she said. "Since I left the physical world, I've stayed around because I still feel strongly responsible for you."

My heart welled up with love and my eyes with tears. I missed her, and her Chaldean Aramaic words, especially *brati*, my daughter. After my mother's death, people said *"Itakh a'jil"* meaning that I had points in heaven for doing good for her. They also told me not to feel sad, that my mother *is* always with me. The ones who said it with conviction had lost one or two of their parents and considered themselves to have gained an angel in heaven who they prayed to.

For decades, I've known that there's more to life than just the physical realm. The moments where I consciously or unconsciously listen to my intuition, I connect to the spiritual world and receive wise directions that otherwise would be unavailable to me, a capacity that is said to be more naturally available to women. In our modern-day society, we tend to devalue our intuitive side, mark it as gullible and deluded, instead of imaginative, creative, instinctive, and highly sensitive, the tribal aspects of humans that have become suppressed by an oversaturated educational system that relies on ever-changing textbooks. In school, we're basically told what to believe and, at the same time, told to be a critical thinker and question everything. But if we question everything, we're judged for that and become a pest.

I observed my mother's face, the eyes that glistened with innocence and the wrinkles that vibrated wisdom. She had strong roots with the ancients, even while living in the modern world. She reminded me of how, without the usage of books, the Sumerians experienced sudden, huge advances in development five thousand years ago, which led them to achieve over one hundred "firsts" for human civilization. Science, medicine, astronomy, schools, and city planning all originated in Sumer. Sumerians invented a wide range of technology, including the wheel, arithmetic, geometry, saws and other tools, the sailboat, chariots, harpoons, sandals, beer, and of course, cuneiform writing.

The invention of writing in Mesopotamia transformed the ancient world, enabling small communities to grow into complex commercial, political, and artistic empires. The oldest surviving writing fragments are clay tablets created 5,300 years ago in Sumer. They used cuneiform, a system of symbols that evolved from pictures (pictograms), and which proved versatile enough for many languages across the region. The earliest writing listed commercial transactions, but soon included legal codes, treaties, historical records, and medical texts. Letters, receipts, hymns, prayers, and stories have all been found on clay tablets. They wrote down their history, created literature and credited the Annunaki, not education for their achievements, leading to a controversial theory of whether or not the human race might have been created, or assisted, in its advancement by extraterrestrial beings in the remote past.

Whether the stories of the Annunaki were mythology or factual, no one really knows, but it's undeniable that the ancients believed in a higher power. Sumerian religion has its foundations in the worship of nature, such as the wind, water, sun, moon, and stars. The forces of nature were originally worshiped as themselves. But over time they believed in one supreme power, the sky beings known as the Annunaki—giant, winged gods, who were said to be connected to the stars and created humans in their image and after their likings. These gods were female and male, immortal and all-powerful, described to have a radiance, an otherworldly feeling about them, but they ate, drank, married, had pets, wrote, etc.

I looked around the land, the sand, and the ancient ruins.

"Why am I here?" I asked.

"Don't give me a headache with all these questions," she said in her customary way.

I had to laugh. This was my mother alright, always matter-of-fact, not wanting to waste time with questions, probably tired of giving answers after giving birth to twelve children. As a daughter, it bothered me that she didn't oblige my curiosity. When I became a mother, I understood her exasperation with questions which required time and reflection to answer. She felt she had little time left on this earth and she did not want to use it to look at the past, the long list of people she loved who were now gone. The future meant the realization of her life coming to an end, when she'd reunite with those loved ones now gone, and miss out on the rest of her children's and grandchildren's lives.

Besides, why was I raising the question of "Why am I here?" to her when I knew the answer? I'm here, visiting my mother in the past, because I want to come closer to the wisdom and legacy of my ancestors, and then bring that wisdom to my people that we both might understand how to live in a good way. To live in a way knowing that death is not something to be feared. To learn about the systems that have gone for too long broken and ineffective. To remember, to give birth to the awareness of why I am on this earth, so that I can have the courage to live my unique brilliance and keep giving my gifts to the world.

I was grateful for this interaction that linked me to a previous civilization and people—my people. Somehow or another I was personally connected to them, to their stories of Adam and Eve, the Flood, Moses, the Garden of Eden—not in a prideful way, but in a way that demands and deserves my attention and that of others. We may live in the twenty-first century, but people came before us and achieved many, many things. These people give us a sense of who we are in history, providing that thread that is missing today and causing a great deal of suffering for humanity, for the youth in particular.

My mother wiped her hands against her mumu and stood. "I will finish making food later," she said. "There are other places for us to see and a lot of important things still to learn. Let me show you."

"What are you making?" I asked, looking at the bowl.

"Piqoota," she said, taking me to the warm and delicious aroma of barley cooked with turmeric, which resided in our kitchen not too long ago when we lived together. In those days, she tried to instill in me the ancient teachings that, back then, I took for granted and resisted.

"These are the pictures of our pioneers," Judy said, pointing to rows of black-and-white photos on the right side of the wall. "And these are the pictures of children that the church provided," she added, pointing to the rows of children's black-and-white photos on the left side of the wall.

I looked up and saw that I was in the "Chaldeans Today" gallery. It was a small room dark rooms with a media monitor that contained interviews with various community members. Adjacent were the following words written vertically on the doorway as one exists the museum: Our Story Continues…

CHAPTER 13

THE LITTLER LITTLE BAGHDAD

One Saturday morning in September, I breathed in the impressions that Henry Ford intended me and others to have when he built Greenfield Village, a collection of nearly a hundred historic buildings that sit on a two-hundred-acre site in Dearborn, another city that's nicknamed "Little Baghdad." The largest Arab population in Dearborn are of Lebanese descent and most are Muslim. I sat at the grounds of Cotswold Cottage, which was built of limestone in England in 1619, dismantled in its birthplace, and re-erected in its new home over three hundred years later.

Tables were set up outside for café hours which seemed to not have started yet. The last time I tried to dine at Cotswold with my daughter, they had closed just before we got here at 4 p.m. Now it's 11 a.m. When do they open? I'd like to have breakfast here, if possible, or lunch, or even just a biscuit.

The nearby roaring sound of Ford's Model T cars passed by, one after another, with the driver explaining, almost shouting, the number of pedals on the wheel, that it only had front and rear windows but no windshield wipers, and no air condition or heat in the car, and so on and so forth. A bee kept whirling around my pen as I wrote in my journal. Sometimes it landed on the lid of my coffee cup, purchased from the gift shop. More and more people began filling the sidewalks as the hours shifted from morning to noon.

I paused from writing to view the scene. *I love this place.*

Dearborn was formed in 1833 and named after patriot Henry Dearborn, a general in the American Revolution who later served as Secretary of War under President Thomas Jefferson. It is home to Michigan's leading tourist attraction, The Henry Ford, the nation's largest indoor-outdoor American history museum entertainment complex. It includes Greenfield Village, the IMAX Theatre, and the Ford Rouge Factory Tours, attracting nearly 1.6 million visitors each year.

The history, the disconnect from a fast-paced life on the outside, the genius behind it, the genius within it. Henry Ford, Thomas Edison, Robert Frost, Noah Webster, Abraham Lincoln—great men whose spirits live within this little town. Do people feel their energy when they visit or are these merely stories of important people and buildings to them? Do they feel the presence of these people? I do. I hear them telling me to keep going forward, to dream big, to allow myself to receive, to embrace my vision, love the hard work, know it'll all come to pass.

After reflecting, I returned to writing in my journal. I really love my life and everyone and everything in it. I feel it's the Garden of Eden that my ancestors once enjoyed before the imbalance that created so much ignorance. Yet there's so much in me that still hasn't been used. I have such tremendous talent, as much if not more than some of the geniuses that reside here in Greenfield Village, none of which, I just realized, are women. Times have changed, of course. Genius women are making their footprints more and more each day. Even women who were overlooked or left out of history are making a comeback.

I love all of that, and know that I will be, Am, one of these women. I am a genius whose name will go on forever. I've helped set a strong foundation for my children, grandchildren, and their children. I've also set a strong foundation for my tribe and community. Narendra, a man from India and my first spiritual teacher, once said that I'm going to do miracles, and he was right, though it's the divine doing these miracles and it's the divine bringing forth the genius with the help of my cooperation.

In the dictionary, the word genius is defined as an "exceptional intellectual or creative power or other natural ability," but really there is no one definition of genius. Many medical experts, spiritual teachers, and individuals believe that geniuses are born as well as made. They share the view that there's a potential genius in everyone that's not yet realized. I'm sure a lot of geniuses go around unnoticed, unaware of their own intelligence as they focus on the knowledge they lack and told by others that they aren't good enough. Maybe they are aware of their own genius, but because no one else believes in them, they make do with what they have and never attain that title, or attain it too late, as is the case with many artists.

Sarah Jordan, a distant cousin of Thomas Edison who ran the 1870 built boarding house that now sits inside Greenfield Village, made the house a home to at least a dozen of Edison's employees. With some help from her daughter and a domestic servant, she organized and coordinated the affair of cleaning, cooking, and doing the laundry to care for these men. Doesn't it take a lot of genius to do that? And what about Vivian Maier, who was obsessed with street photography. Born in 1926, she spent forty years as a nanny. Everyone thought she was peculiar, and no one had a clue of her talents until 2007 when her work was discovered at a local thrift auction house by John Maloof. He became obsessed with Vivian's work and made it his mission to re-construct her archive which included nearly 150,000 negatives, hundreds of rolls of film, home movies, audio tape interviews, and other items. Sadly, Vivian died in 2009 before John brought her work to the public eye.

The bright sun, constant sound of train engine, colorful flowers, and the large fruit tree behind me, freed me of negative emotions. It was like bathing in a tub of inspiration and enthusiasm that would soon travel, if it hadn't done so already, to those I live with, causing a shift, a sense of freedom for them as well. *I love it here.* I came that morning because I'd worked hard all week, and this was my reward, my date with self. To sit inside Greenfield Village and write in my journal, to remember my dream, to remember I'm living it. With new zest, I soaked in the beautiful scenery around me. Was that a lemon tree behind me? Many black lemons were scattered on the floor, a few still green. It was probably a walnut tree.

"All aboard!" the train conductor called out, followed by a Model T driver who, passing by, asked the passengers, "What is three hundred plus three hundred? It's five hundred…" *Five hundred what?* I wanted to ask, but the car was too loud and the train too far by now for me to have heard the answer. My attention returned to the cottage. I had read that it was brought along with Cotswold sheep and doves. Ford thought the impression was incomplete without a sheepdog, so "Rover" was bought for $75 who "protected the few sheep around and he was the master of that whole place."

Soon I began strolling through the homes and buildings of the families who founded this nation that Ford wanted us to know about, who they were, how they lived. Look what money could do! But money without freedom could only get you so far. We came here with nothing, ran away from harm, but no matter how rich we become, we won't be able to find the home we left behind. When I visited Iraq in 2000, the owners of my childhood home refused to let me inside.

I decided to get on a horse carriage. The driver, Emma, told me she was riding the only two female horses at the premises: Catherine and Abigale. The other seventeen horses were males.

"I love my job," she said.

"I can imagine," I said. "I've wanted to, or thought of, getting a job here so I can hang out on these grounds."

"The job doesn't pay much, starting at $12 an hour for carriage drivers," she admitted, "but we really need the help."

The pay didn't matter. The idea of breaking away from my daily routine and being amongst history, nature, horses, wrapped up in stories, was appealing. Working in the past, in old-fashioned settings, and visiting homes where the spirits of the geniuses resided, would be temporary, of course, until my life journey developed.

I moved on, enjoying the unpaved roads, wondering why there wasn't a hotel inside Greenfield Village where I could stay for a night or two or three. To really step back in time and absorb the energy of the originality and creativity here, ironically built by a man who was quoted to have said that "history is more or less bunk." But who cares what he said? He provided a historical experience that inspired and enthralled millions of people around the world. The sights and sounds of a traditional rural America and its virtues of self-reliance, hard work and prudence, of learning by doing, trials and errors, suited my heart, which yearned to recreate the physical surroundings of my girlhood and that of my ancestors.

And anyway, over the years many clarifications, interpretations, and speculations about Ford's quote have left people with their own conclusions to what he really meant. My favorites were that Ford was simply "trying to keep mankind from getting bogged down in the past." He was also saying that "History, taught in textbooks, focused far too much on kings and battles and far too little on how the common man lived." But honestly, I doubt anyone can really comprehend the context of Ford's statement, given the passage of time, and the fact that history means different things to different people.

Greenfield Village opened to the public in 1933, the year my mother was born, and over seventy years later, the Arab American National Museum (AANM) opened in the same city. AANM is the first and only museum devoted to Arab American history and culture. It was originally a furniture store that took four years to build into a museum. The museum, decorated on the front with opulent turquoise tiles and geometric patterns, is crowned with a dome that makes it look like a mosque, but it is non-denominational.

The first floor includes the contributions of the Arab civilization to science, medicine, architecture, decorative arts, and mathematics. The second floor focuses on the immigration story and how prominent Arab Americans such as Ralph Nader and Helen Thomas contributed to America. The third floor is reserved for administration, and the lower level is the auditorium where in 2010 I displayed a work-in-process portion of my feature documentary, *The Great American Family*.

One day I visited the AANM with a group of women that included friends and family, along with my daughter. Our tour guide was Rafat, who I happened to have met years ago. I also knew his brother through the various cultural and educational events we attended.

Rafat was friendly, kind, and informative. He told us about his upcoming travels, that he was going to Tunisia and other Arab countries, and yes, he insisted upon seeing some of our arched brows, it's safe to go visit those regions. Looking at our group, I realized I was the only person born in an Arab country. Probably the only one who knew the classic Arabic songs and movies that I tucked away in my memory after my mother's passing. A favorite was *The Cup Reader* by legendary Egyptian singer Abdel Halim Hafez with lyrics written by Nizar Qabbani:

She sat with fear in her eyes
Contemplating the upturned cup
She said "Do not be sad, my son
You are destined to fall in love."

In silence, I bowed out of the docent-led tour and entered a deep trance of joy and sadness, to a time when my siblings and I were very affectionate and more expressive with each other. We laughed to the point of rolling on the floor and spluttering unfathomable words. We cried openly and naturally in ways that stoic cultures do not. Daily we enjoyed delicious homecooked meals and on holidays more elaborate ones. At celebrations, we let loose, drawn to the dance floor by emotional and exotic melodies. Nothing could stop us. Whether it was *khigga*, line dancing, or *raqis sharqi*, eastern dance (otherwise known as belly dancing), we got into the sensual, not sexual, movements. It was all so magical.

"Religion is the bread and butter of the Arab world," said Rafat, bringing me to reality, to the very topic that has destroyed the magic of that land. "The three monolithic religions of that region are Judaism, Christianity, and Islam. There are different religions as well; Mandeans are gnostic, and with it, you cannot convert."

Rafat is Mandean, which I hadn't known before. There is an estimated sixty to seventy thousand Mandeans worldwide, a closed ethno-religious community. Also known as Sabeans, they originate from ancient Mesopotamia, although some believe they are one of the "Lost Tribes of Israel" who fled from the Jordan Valley to the Tigris and Euphrates during the Judeo-Roman war in 66 AD. It's also possible that when the Babylonians invaded Jerusalem in 597 BC, many Jews and Mandeans were taken to Babylon as either prisoners of war or skilled citizens.

Mandeans don't believe in prophets and trace their roots to John the Baptist, not as followers but descendants. As such, they are related to his cousin, Jesus of Nazareth. They consider themselves the original Baptists and allow people to get baptized as many times as they want, preferring to do the water ritual in the river since its water comes from heaven. They are the only gnostic religion that has survived, with a common belief in salvation by knowledge and freedom of religion. They don't believe there is a "holy land" or a "chosen people" and they are against engaging in fighting over anything, including land.

"Religions of the past were not missionary religions," said Rafat. "People didn't try to convert each other. Do you know how many denominations there are of Christianity?"

We made various guesses, and the correct answer was thirty-three thousand. What's with all the thirty-three? The age I was when my first book was published and during the same time I got engaged. My father changed gravesites after thirty-three years. Jesus' traditional age when he was crucified and resurrected. According to Al-Ghazali, a Persian Imam, the dwellers of Heaven will exist eternally in a state of being age thirty-three. Islamic prayer beads are usually organized in sets of thirty-three. This number for many people is associated with charisma and abundance, and it also represents power and growth. The *Divine Comedy*, an Italian poem by Dante Alighieri which he began in 1308 and completed a year before his death in 1320, deals with thirty-three miners who were trapped underground for thirty-three days, but survive. Age thirty-three is the best year of our lives, a new survey has found. A British website, *Friends Reunited*, says that 70 percent of people over forty picked that age as their happiest.

Rafat went on to explain that there are two main Muslim sects: the Shia and the Sunni. These two sects agree on most of the fundamental beliefs and practices of Islam. The bitter divide between them that started some fourteen centuries ago, however, is based on who they believe should succeed Prophet Muhammad as leader of the Islamic faith. The Shia believed Muhammad's teachings should be followed by a blood relative, his cousin Ali, after his death. The Sunni believed the religion's leader should be chosen by its followers. This dispute fractured many countries in the Middle East, including Iraq and Syria.

"What's the difference between being religious and spiritual?" someone asked.

"Religion is knowing the text and following it," he said. "Spirituality is interpreting the text and applying it to what suits your needs and growth through your interpretation; spirituality is in every religion."

We somehow got on the topic of Sufism, and my ears and heart perked up. I was introduced to this mystical form of Islam almost thirty years ago by my first spiritual teacher, Narendra. One day, he handed me an 822-page book called *Daughter of Fire: A Diary of a Spiritual Training with a Sufi Master* and said, "Read this. It'll answer a lot of your questions."

I gobbled up the book within a week or so. It was about the Russian-born widow Irina Tweedie who had a background in Theosophy. In 1961, at age fifty-four, she went from England to India to study under a Sufi Master. He asked her to write a diary about her experience. In the book, Irina emphasizes the daily details that sometimes feel strenuous to read, forcing you to stand still as you witness her letting go of her ego. The process occurs in seven stages in which she kills her worldly desires to merge into oneness with all things past, present, and future. The diary was such a deep dive into the requirements of the initiate for the transformation of human consciousness to experience God, that in later years I re-read it from beginning to end. I have since used it for spiritual comfort and reference.

However, none of the women friends who I recommended

this book to were able to read it past a few pages. One was disturbed by how the Sufi Master treated Irina and another felt it was simply too tedious and repetitive. But isn't that what the spiritual path is, and why so many people are deterred from it?

"Are Mandeans allowed to marry outside of their community?" someone else asked, pulling me away from the dreamlike Sufi practices embedded in the sacred ritual chanting of God's attributes and mystical dancing, such as that performed by the whirling dervishes.

"If a man or woman marries a non-Mandean, their children will not be considered to be Mandeans," he responded.

"Do you think that's right, though?" she asked, and the group broke up into different conversations as he addressed her question and we sauntered to the second floor. There, we took a picture in front of a map of the Arab World which consists of twenty-two countries: ten in Africa and twelve in Asia. A common thing these countries have in common, he pointed out, is the Arabic language, but normally the mother tongue is different. All are part of the Arab League.

"Animism is the indigenous religion from Africa," he said. We'd somehow bounced back to the topic of religion. "Ethiopia has a lot of different religions living together."

Rafat changed topics to get us thinking about the early immigration. Zammouri was the first recorded Arabic speaker to come to North America. His name means "someone from Zammour" and Zammouri is the city in Morocco where he was born over five hundred years ago. He was likely captured in 1511 by the Portuguese, then sold into slavery. His captors renamed him Estebanico, and after sixteen years, he was taken to Florida as part of a Spanish expeditionary force.

"We consider Zammouri Arabic because he spoke Arabic," Rafat said, "but we don't know what he considered himself because as mentioned earlier, there were many different groups from that region who are classified as indigenous but can also speak Arabic. We don't know if he had a mother-tongue."

He explained that Arabs have been immigrating to the United States in waves beginning in the 1800s. The first wave was in 1860, mostly Christian Syrians from Great Syria. The second wave of Arabs came in the 1930s and 1940s having been displaced from Palestine. They went to New York where they commonly worked as peddlers. Many brought their house keys, thinking one day, they would return to their homes.

"There was a brain drain in that region," he said. "Programs encouraged intellectuals to leave their countries and come to the west."

"Doesn't the Arab world have its own inner brain drain where they get rid of all their intellectuals?" I asked.

"Yeah, that too," he said.

"My father grew up in Lebanon," one of our group members said. "His father kidnapped him from Iraq and took him there…"

Rafat's eyes widened as the young lady went on to tell him her father's life story, or the most dramatic part of it. At some point, he took control again and said, "The Middle East is a term coined by the Europeans. It's a geographic term. We identify ourselves as Middle Eastern, but the term is not correct. 'Middle East' is the name given to the region in 1901 by the British."

Our tour soon turned into lively conversations, as we discussed what Arabs are known for—hospitality, faith, and family. In her thesis *Second-Generation Experiences of Ethnicity: Chaldean American Women in Metro-Detroit*, Sandy Naimou writes that all the women she spoke to identify family cohesion as one of the positive qualities of Chaldean culture, adding, "They depict family centrality and cohesion as the major characteristic, cultural marker, and asset of Chaldean culture." The flip coin is that this type of family cohesion results in so much obligatory work that many women also felt held back by family. I would argue that this is the case for Middle Easterners in general.

When the tour ended, we asked if he could suggest a Yemini restaurant and coffee shop. At his suggestion, we walked to Sheeba Restaurant for lunch, the name referring to a kingdom mentioned in the Old Testament and the Quran. The hot fresh flatbread and spicy flaming flavors mixed into stews, sauces, and rice made our heads whirl. Afterward, we headed to Haraz Coffee House, named after the mountains known for growing coffee beans and *qat*, a flowering plant that contains a stimulant. The specialty coffees with milk, cardamom and nutmeg were no less effective and almost set us off into a whirling dance.

We had a lovely time. Like Sterling Heights, this city reminds me of home with its ethnic grocery stores, restaurants, and mosques. It makes me smile and love it more for all its quirky Arab attributes, many which resemble that of the Chaldeans, with stores translated to the owner's liking. The Arabic signate Al Riyadh Market that's translated to Papaya Fruit Market in English; the Arabic Al Mustafa Market that's translated to Greenland Market in English.

At home, I did some research on Google and discovered an article titled *The Mandaeans: True Descendants of Ancient Babylonians and Chaldeans*, written in 2002 by historian Fredrick Aprim. He observed that this community, just like their forefathers, the Babylonians, had a special interest in the study of astronomy and mathematics. They preserved major elements of the ancient Chaldean religion, including the sacred ritual of giving newborns astrological names or names of the sign of the Zodiac. Their holy books and spoken language are in Mandaic, a form of Aramaic.

I sighed, heavily. The past is a beautiful place that I like to dwell in, playing it over and over again like a favorite movie, but no matter how I remember it, it's gone. I don't want to be stuck in the past, but I do enjoy playing with nostalgia while I write, direct, and edit my present and future story, rewriting the chapters and scenes that will produce the next book, the film, of my inner reality. Reading poetry brings forth the sweet nostalgia I once had for my birthland and Rumi captures that feeling in his poem, "Only Breath."

> *Not Christian or Jew or Muslim, not Hindu*
> *Buddhist, Sufi, or Zen. Not any religion*
> *or cultural system. I am not from the East*
> *or the West, not out of the ocean or up*
> *from the ground, not natural or ethereal, not*
> *composed of elements at all. I do not exist,*
> *am not an entity in this world or in the next,*
> *did not descend from Adam and Eve or any*
> *origin story. My place is placeless, a trace*
> *of the traceless. Neither body or soul.*
> *I belong to the beloved, have seen the two*
> *worlds as one and that one call to and know,*
> *first, last, outer, inner, only that*
> *breath breathing human being.*

CHAPTER 14

LEARNING ARAMAIC

The warmth of the crackling flames beside me, I lean against the marble fireplace hearth and, despite the loud television in the background that my husband is watching, I read a book by Father Michael Bazzi. *The Life of Tilkepnaye* was written in three languages—English, Aramaic-Chaldean, and Arabic, "for the benefit of the old and the young," the author states in the beginning pages. Born in northern Iraq in the beautiful town of Tilkepe (the way he spells it), Father Bazzi was ordained a Catholic priest in Baghdad in 1964. He later moved to Rome where he earned a master's degree in Pastoral Theology from Lateran University, taking along the soil of his birth town wherever he traveled. He came to the United States in 1974 and began serving as a priest in the Green Bay Diocese in Wisconsin. He also began what was to become a lifelong love of teaching the Scriptures and the Aramaic language by teaching workshops throughout the region. He authored ten books, five of which focus on the Aramaic language, and since 1989 has taught Aramaic at Cuyamaca College in El Cajon, San Diego where there's a strip on Main Street called "Little Baghdad." That nickname is also given to an area in Texas where the movie *Baghdad Texas* was filmed. None of those regions compare to the "Little Baghdad" that exists in Sterling Heights.

Between the college and his parish, Father Bazzi taught more than a hundred Aramaic students a year. He is now retired but still sleeps with the soil he brought with him from Tilkepe placed under his pillow.

I pet Teddy, who lies beside me, and sigh. In my office desk drawer, I too have soil from my birthplace of Baghdad, which my brother-in-law brought me in a plastic bag when he came home from serving in the U.S. Army as a translator. I grew up speaking, reading, and writing Arabic. I completely understood Aramaic, its Chaldean dialect, which my parents, older siblings, and relatives spoke. I did not speak it. If someone asked *"Dikhiwat?"* (How are you?) in Aramaic, I responded, *"Zayna"* (Fine) in Arabic. Most of the time we would continue communicating in this fashion, but sometimes an elderly person would ask me, *"Lakithat id-mahikyat Sureth?"* (You don't know how to speak Aramaic?)

I know how to, but not too good, I'd explain, leaving out the part that I feared making a fool of myself by mispronouncing words. I could see their surprise, in some cases even their disappointment, not at me but at the situation. In Iraq, Christians were persecuted on an ethnic, cultural, and racial level. While most of them speak Aramaic, reading and writing that language was both suppressed by outer policies and repressed by inner fears. True, Christians under Saddam Hussein's regime were tolerated. As a matter of fact, Saddam's deputy Tariq Aziz was a Christian. Yet he changed his distinctly Christian birth name, Mikhail Yuhanna, to the more Arabic sounding Tariq Aziz to gain acceptance by the Arab and Muslim majority.

Aramaic, one of the oldest spoken languages, is an early Semitic language that predates Hebrew and Arabic. It is in danger of becoming a dead language. During the latter half of the first millennium BC, Aramaic was the common language of most of the Near East and the official administrative language of the powerful Assyrian, Babylonian, and Persian empires. It was essentially an international language before such a thing existed. People used it for commerce and government across territory stretching from Egypt and the Holy Land to India and China. As Jesus died on the cross, he cried in Aramaic, *"Elahi, Elahi, lema shabaqtani?"* (My God, my God, why have you forsaken me?)

The Aramaic speakers who looked at me with surprise or disappointment did so because they wanted to preserve the language, and the only way they could do that was with the younger generation's participation. Aramaic is down to its last generation or two of speakers, most of them scattered over the past century from homelands where their language once flourished. In their new lands, few children and even fewer grandchildren learn it. This generational rupture marks a language's last days. Unfortunately, the reality is that sometimes due to circumstances one is deprived of the opportunities to know or learn one's native language. My parents, for instance, had the burdensome task of escaping an authoritarian regime and, as minorities, had to keep a low profile.

Teddy nudges closer beside me, his body now rubbing against my thigh, and falls into a deeper slumber. I crumble ads and throw them into the fireplace to rekindle the fire. I then look further into this language through an internet search. Over three millennia of continuous records exist for Aramaic. For many religions, this language has had sacred or near-sacred status. It survived until the twentieth century shattered what remained of it. During World War I, as the Ottoman power dissolved, Turkish nationalists not only massacred Armenians, Assyrians, Chaldeans, and Greeks, but also perpetrated what is known today as the Sayfo Genocide, slaughtering and expelling the Christian Aramaic-speaking population of eastern Turkey. Most survivors fled to Iran and Iraq. A few decades later, facing rising anti-Semitism, most Jewish Aramaic speakers left for Israel. Ayatollah Khomeini's Iran and Saddam Hussein's Iraq added further pressures and persecutions for the Aramaic-speaking Christians who stayed behind.

Before the Gulf War in 1991, Chaldeans numbered about one million. By the time of the US-led invasion in 2003, that figure had fallen to approximately 800,000. The spread of ISIS forces across northern Iraq has resulted in widespread displacement of the community and the destruction of its cultural and religious heritage, sites, and property. Following the group's takeover of Mosul in June 2014, many Chaldeans fled the city along with other minorities. Diaspora became a fact of life for the Christian Iraqis, most of who now live scattered across the globe, from countries bordering the former Aramaic-speaking zone like Turkey, Jordan, and Russia, to newer communities in places like Michigan, California, and the Chicago suburbs. Those who came to the U.S. settled mostly in Michigan, where their ancestors have lived since the early twentieth century and where the largest concentration of Chaldeans in the world live, with a population of over 180,000.

I took a sip of my hot chocolate, came closer to the fire, opened Father Bazzi's book, and read the following chant in Aramaic:

Oh Tilkepe, you are honey in my mouth.
Your name I bear within me.
Oh land of my father and mother
Your soil I mix with my blood.

Old memories rushed toward me once again, stinging me a bit. A combination of good and bad old days that made me who I am today, they were of things and people that I wish were still in my life but no longer were a part of my life. My mind was drawn to the dancing flames and its hypnotic effect.

The longer it remained there, the more I partook of the wisdom of my mother, the one who gave birth to me, those who attended to my spiritual and instinctual needs, those who protected me, and the Great Mother, the Earth.

The flames washed over the mumbo jumbo of this hectic world and brought forth ideas my father, a progressive man, might have shared, if we had had those conversations. I imagine that, in regard to language, he would've thought that if your family is settled away from your native region for generations where another language is spoken, you start speaking the latter as your mother tongue at home. You don't even think about the former language that was brought by your distant ancestors. My father would probably have voted for the world to unite and create a common language that would make international communication significantly easier. People would be more open and prone to international collaboration and less prejudice.

Had I entertained that conversation, I would have agreed with my father. I'm a lot like him, ardently interested in my work and having a desire to serve the world, to "cast my bread upon the waters." If tomorrow we were all silenced, we'd survive as a species. We would find another way to communicate, and it might not be verbally. Even though I would have agreed with him, I also believe that culture gives us a strong sense of belonging and a sense of purpose; that erasing one's culture or imposing one's ways through force, violence, and destruction is extremely harmful.

In 2019, I accepted a position at the Chaldean Cultural Center, the non-profit organization that created the mysterious Chaldean Museum that the French filmmakers were denied but I eventually experienced first-hand. Since I started working there, every day I am faced with the idea that this community's cultural identity is endangered. I feel it is especially important to shed light on its existence by systematizing the memories of its people. With factors like poverty, disease, old age, and displacement, it often feels that time is running out. And with the last survivors of the oral memory of the group, particularly the elderly, dying, it's essential to preserve their language and stories. While I don't want to participate in a race, so consumed with the end that I'm unable to enjoy the present, I also don't want the present to become an expiration date. I want to see this language move along and have a position in the world, the way the Jews have taken care of their Hebrew language, despite all circumstances.

I recalled two specific incidents that pushed me to pursue the documentation and preservation of this language. I was visiting the library archivist at the Holocaust Memorial Center. Her husband was an expert in the Talmud. Certain parts of the Bible were written in Aramaic, such as the books of Daniel and Ezra, as was the Babylonian and Jerusalem Talmuds. Yet she had no clue that Chaldeans still spoke Aramaic. She was stunned and so was I, both of us for different reasons. Another time I was translating for a young Yemini Muslim woman at a hospital, one whose name was Ingeel (Bible). They were absolutely surprised to hear I spoke a different language, one that belonged to Christians. They asked me to speak, and I did, and they were in awe. They reminded me of the time my husband's friend took him for his relatives to view "a Christian," which they'd never seen before.

"Teddy is by the fence" says a text, interrupting my thoughts. I look and notice that Teddy is no longer beside me. Someone had let him out in the midst of the snow, his favorite playground. Engrossed in my research, I ask my son, "Can you give Teddy to the neighbors?" He complains, given the mounds of snow he must walk through in his sandals.

I return my attention to the fire and ask it this important

question, in the unspoken language that the fire and I are accustomed to, which favors the English translation: from this moment on, how will I invest my seconds, hours, and days with the rest of my unlived life before it too becomes a memory? This is precisely why I am here. I have come to make things right, to use my position, along with others, to inspire humanity to take an interest in preserving and documenting our stories and language.

So I made friends with people of similar interests who showed up at my door. Roy Gessford is a non-Chaldean who is so dedicated to preserving the Chaldean language that for some time he moved to Michigan from California. In his book *Preserving the Chaldean Aramaic Language*, Gessford writes, "The preservation of Aramaic will be especially useful to future generations in understanding the deeper meaning of sacred religious and historical documents written in Aramaic and Semitic languages related to Aramaic such as Hebrew and Arabic."

Roy introduced me to a number of scholars including Professor Khan, Father Michael Bazzi, and Dr. Rocco Errico, one of the nation's leading Biblical scholars working from the original Aramaic Peshitta texts. In my own community, I met Mahir Awrahem, who has several masters' degrees, teaches Aramaic, and has authored a book and done audio lessons on Mango about the topic. After we met, he began the first Aramaic language class at the Chaldean Cultural Center. It's so successful that since it started it has been ongoing. Similarly to Roy, these teachers and scholars state the importance of preserving the Aramaic language.

I never imagined ending up in a job that made it necessary to be fluent in Aramaic. If only I had started learning this language earlier in life. Instead, I invested years into learning French and, while I passed with flying colors, I barely learned more than "Comment allez vous?" and "Parlez vous Francais?"

These phrases got me an "A" in class but I doubt they would do me much good when lost in the streets of France, not that if I were lost in the streets of France I'd actually want to find my way.

Back then, I had big dreams about traveling to Europe. I checked out foreign films from libraries or watched them at the Detroit Institute of Film. I bought books about Italy, France, Greece, along with a map of major European cities and restaurant guides. I was more fascinated about other cultures than my own, until a series of events led me to Arab countries, to memories of my old world, to wanting to reconnect with my heritage.

After I received my bachelor's degree from Wayne State University, I began my travels around the world and each time I returned home, I tiptoed around topics related to my ancestry. St. Joseph Chaldean Catholic Church provided Aramaic evening classes in the 1990s. I registered and received a book titled *Chaldean Reading Book* by Mary Yousif. It included the Aramaic alphabet and some basic words such as cat, goose, bell, and treasure. It was a nice class for beginners but not exactly one that helped me become fluent in speaking, reading, and writing Aramaic.

I had all the tools to make me fluent in this language—a family and community that spoke it fluently and a class for beginners, not to mention full comprehension. Then what was the resistance? I suppose that as long as my mother was alive, it felt close and intimate and a part of me. Once she was gone, its absence woke me up to its value.

After she passed away, I began to understand the important role that Aramaic played in antiquity, and what a linguistic and cultural treasure it is. I was no longer satisfied understanding the language. I wanted to speak it. Love goes a long way when you begin to understand your roots. But when I attempted to do so, I noticed it wasn't as easy as I thought. Aside from practice, loads and loads of practice, it required an adequate amount of confidence. Committing to practice was doable but acquiring confidence was questionable. In this particular case, the language carried traumatic experiences within its fabric.

After three thousand years, the Aramaic language lost its standing in that region in the seventh century AD when Muslim armies from Arabia conquered the area, establishing Arabic as the key tongue. Aramaic survived in remote areas such as the Kurdish areas of Turkey, Iraq, Iran, and Syria. The political and religious situations caused many people from that region to carry inside of them buried traumas, confusion, frustration, embarrassment, or even shame.

My people have for a long time suffered from different types of persecutions in their native land of Mesopotamia, including numerous genocides. As Christians we were considered infidels and given the option to either convert to Islam, be killed, or pay *jizya*, a tax. This was called "Ah-Dhimma" or the "People under Protection." Individuals could escape this second-class citizen status by doing two things: switch their native language to Arabic or convert to Islam. Many took the offer, so the distinct ethnicities of the Middle East became absorbed into a newly expanding Arab ethnicity.

This was the way of our ancestors for over fifteen hundred years, the severity depending on the time and group. Many were killed, but many converted to Islam and melted into the inhabitants of the given region, inhabitants such as the Arabs, Kurds, and Persians. Over time, they abandoned their language and forgot their origin. Communities who resisted converting to Islam had to watch their civilization dragged back into the Stone Age. Through this process, their hatred for the term "Arab" was established. In the case of Chaldeans, they are proud to be of the few minorities in the Middle East who succeeded in maintaining their religion and language. Those living in a diaspora, scattered across the world, have much of the same sentiments.

Unlike the Jewish genocides, these atrocities have been, and still are, brushed under a carpet. People refuse to go through the trouble of getting a dustpan to sweep up the dirt of the past. The negative experiences of the past damaged and outweighed the positive ones, so people felt insecure, uncertain, or nervous about speaking Aramaic. This prevented some from continuing to speak and pass on their mother tongue.

Maybe I soaked in those feelings of shame and insecurities when trying to speak the language, and therefore felt a sense of judgment, lack, or fear. But here we are, decades later, on a land where we are able to re-cultivate a positive experience about the Aramaic language, and maybe even preserve it. We're also on a land where we can recognize that semitic groups are quite distinct from Arabs but acknowledge as well, that we have been mixed and assimilated with Arab societies, culture, language, customs, and traditions for fifteen hundred years. After all, many are hooked to their Arabic soap operas and news channels, pay big bucks to go to concerts of famous Arabic singers, and jump onto the dance floor with Arab friends to join them in line dance, *dapke*, or belly dance.

The flames continued to cause a hypnotic effect. It was so mesmerizing and pretty. In this non-distracting, peaceful state, I took refuge. I then received a text: "Teddy is ready to go home." It was typed in English between two Chaldean people who are fluent in Aramaic, Arabic, and English. The letter "A" is alep in Aramaic; alif in Arabic; A in English, now the official universal language that these two women have adopted, and they are good with that.

CHAPTER 15

THE UPTON HOUSE

One winter day, I decided to visit the past, to once again explore the land that has been my peoples' sanctuary for four decades, and to once again understand its connection to my thousands-year-old lineage which no longer exists in the land I was born in. So I picked up the phone and made a call to reserve a guided tour of the Upton House Museum. Since it was built in 1866, the Upton House has stood on the same site, in plain view of the twenty-first century, its green door open on Wednesday and Sunday afternoons for history-loving patrons, one of whom happens to be me. Certainly, William and Sarah Aldrich Upton never imagined that over a hundred years after they built the classic Victorian Italianate style house, the city of Sterling Heights would purchase it in the late 1970s and begin efforts to preserve it.

It would've been beyond the Upton's wildest dreams to imagine that one day, their descendants, along with city officials, cultural and historical commissioners, Friends of the Upton House, and residents would gather for the open house. That the house would become a registered Michigan historical landmark open to the public. That the public would have such invested interest in this house, they would visit it, write about it, and renovate it. That a woman born more than six thousand miles away in the ancient city of Baghdad would end up in this newer city and take a particular fascination to this house. And she would decide to write about it in one of the chapters in her book.

My husband and I and our teenage daughter and son arrived at the house on a warm and sunny December afternoon. The life size four-hundred-pound bronze statue of Sarah Upton teaching needlepoint to her granddaughter, Sarah Jeanette Upton, stood before us. A woman, a real one and not a statue, awaited us at the front porch, wearing a mask. The man chatting with her said a few last words and then walked away. She greeted us afterward and welcomed us inside the cozy, Christmas-decorated home. Immediately I was transported into another world, as if I'd stepped into a movie, one of those based on Jane Austen's books or Margret Mitchel's *Gone with the Wind,* or Laura Ingles' *Little House on the Prairie* series.

The Victorian-style furniture brought to life an image of the parents sitting on the white upholstered settee, what we call in the US a sofa, with gold and red stripes. The four children were spread out, some sitting on the wooden two-seat rocking chair, and others on the navy, maroon, and gold patterned rug that was 100 percent wool, handmade in India in the twenty-first century. Someone must have sat for hours in front of the old-fashioned pump organ which my son tried to play, but only struck a few notes before leaving it. His foot found the pedals a bit difficult to use.

We felt like semi-giants in this home, considered lavish and large for the typical human back then, when "superfluous flesh," the term used during that era, was never considered a health problem. After all, people worked countless hours on farms and were more likely to lose weight than gain it. The short legs on certain chairs were meant to accommodate women, who would have been wearing stiff corsets, to interact with small children without bending over and to make breast-feeding more comfortable.

A dress at the Upton House, modeled after an 1875 gown on display at the Metropolitan Museum of Art, reminded me of Scarlett O'Hara, supposedly a fictitious character. The labor Scarlett would have gone through to get dressed and then carry that weight around like a sack of potatoes! A full outfit of that time consisted of linen shift, the corset, petticoats, padded waist rolls, stockings, garters, separate pockets, and kerchiefs. With their list of to-dos and the required effort to get dressed and undressed, how did Jane Austen and Laura Ingles have time at the end of the day to write, especially without electricity, relying mostly on gas lamps and candles for light? How did women like Scarlett manage to juggle beauty, children, wars, and farm work when there were no cars and people walked, travelled by boat or train or used coach horses to move from place to place?

My family and I entered the small kitchen and my empathy for those women doubled, though my love for that era didn't diminish. True they didn't have refrigerators and relied on insulated wooden boxes, known as ice boxes, to hold blocks of ice and keep the food cool. A drip pan collected the melt water and had to be emptied daily. But the minimalist and practical sense gave a cozy, simple, and quiet feeling, the very things I thirst for, the things that resembled my childhood home in Iraq. There are kitchens with no appliances that exist even today in villages tucked far away, like in the mountains of Morocco, where once, my friend and I were served mint tea by Berber women. But here there was china from the early 1900s, elaborate beautiful china.

Our tour guide pointed out a metal wash boiler stand painted silver with two gas burners. This essential modern household item was used to heat water for laundry washdays, the occasional baths, cleaning the house, plucking poultry, canning, etc. It reminded me of how my mother, who'd birthed twelve children and buried two, did the washing by filling a large tub with water. She added the traditional bar of olive oil soap, and then scrubbed and wrung each article of clothing before hanging it on a clothesline to dry.

"You can go upstairs to the second floor," our tour guide said, awakening me from the dream of the past, of the simplistic lifestyle where people did what they needed to do to survive, thrive and be productive every day. True, the work was arduous, but the principles people lived by, such as love, respect, perseverance, honor, humility, bravery, sacrifice, generosity, and wisdom, caused less boredom and more satisfaction. Many people today are running for nothing.

"Mom, come on," my son said, observing my trance as he headed toward the stairs.

"Coming," I said, thinking of these women's struggles in a man's world, and how their moral and physical resilience created an overall good life. *I think!*

Time is surreal, available for us to use however we desire to arrange it. We can stack it vertically like cards or set it up horizontally like dominos. We can explore time, be obsessed with time, or become time. With a flick of a finger, we can shorten it or widen it or destroy it. We can romanticize it, if it helps us live a more romantic life. The Mesopotamians, who watched the sun, the moon, the transit of the stars, knew its utmost power. They demonstrated this in the sophisticated ways they created to measure time, strengthening "time" as a concept. They divided time units into sixty parts, which eventually led to sixty-second minutes and sixty-minute hours. Transported to the ancients' wisdom, welcoming their distant yet close voices, I took a few deep breaths before I followed my family to the second floor.

The house had four bedrooms, making it lavish for that time period. The farm initially consisted of 136 acres of property which originally included the footprint of Stephenson High School and part of Dodge Park Road. Over the years, various owners took over the property and its home. They extensively renovated and remodeled the interior. Except for two items, a lamp and a dollhouse displayed on the second floor, most of the objects and furniture were reproductions or donated by people outside the Upton family.

The hurricane-style white and blue cylindrical lamp with an image of a woman in a green dress was donated by the Upton's great-great-granddaughter, Louis Ullrich. The lamp's decorated glass shield would protect the wick flame from drafts. In 1914, Ed Upton built his daughter, Maud, a blue, two story, wooden dollhouse that included cloth dolls and furniture. On the first floor to the left is a blond-haired man sitting at the piano, to the right is a picnic table with benches, with stairs at the back of the house. On the second floor there's a bed, a rocking chair, and other bedroom accessories. Maud asked that it be donated to a historical society, children's museum, or other organization. The family donated it to the Sterling Heights Public Library so that it would remain near the family homestead. When the Upton House was turned into a museum, the family asked that the dollhouse be displayed there.

I looked closely at the dollhouse with awe. Anytime I listen to or read about the history of a building, home, or a large family heirloom such as a kitchen item, fire art, or quilt, I wonder what it feels like to *not have fled* from your birth country. What is it like to be born and raised on your native land? Maybe even the same land as your parents and grandparents, so that when you gather around the fire, sit at the dinner table, go on long drives, or visit relative's homes, you tell stories of what happened in dwellings and streets you are all familiar with. All we brought with us were stories and memories.

In one room were wooden school desks that looked just

like the ones in Walnut Grove church and school. Early in 1845 a group of Sterling Township farmers, feeling the need for an educational facility, met to organize a School District. By the end of the year, a payment of $70 was made out for the building of the schoolhouse. The first teacher was paid $28 per month, considered high, but it came with a price. During her term of contract, a teacher could not marry, keep company with men, had to be home between the hours of 8 p.m. and 6 a.m. unless attending a school function, and could not loiter downtown in ice cream stores. She was not permitted to travel beyond the city limits unless she had permission from the chairman of the board; couldn't ride in a carriage or automobile with any member unless he was her father or brother; could not smoke cigarettes; under no circumstance could she dye her hair; she had to wear at least two petticoats; her dress could not be any shorter than two inches above the ankles. These restrictions reminded me of the regions in the Middle East where women risk their lives to defect to a safer place. And maybe to their surprise, they discover they have to follow similar restrictions on their behavior to earn respect in the immigrant community. Some even choose that way of life, afraid of change or the idea of liberation.

The walls of the Upton House continued to speak to me, to tell me that yes, while many things have changed and evolved, some things are still the same. But it was time to leave. Our tour was scheduled for forty-five minutes, and I could feel my children's attention span reaching its peak. I, on the other hand, wanted to spend the night in that house. Although there was no bed, there was a nice Victorian couch. This would be a perfect place to write in my journal, to express that I loved this place, the stillness, history, and the sense of no rushing. Best of all, I loved that no one else was there, especially those who pretend that the green dots and streaks splattered on a canvas are high art, turning up their noses at the common people who enjoy works of art that stir the emotions. I wanted to take it all in, and through this house, continue my trip into the past, to know that others have walked in my shoes but at different times. Their stories mattered and their work outlasted their lives.

"Mom, can we go now?" came the question I knew my son had patiently awaited, but could no longer wait, to ask.

"Yes," I said and told our docent that next time, I would return by myself. In doing so, I would more deeply romanticize these experiences, thus generating the optimism that makes the world go round. I bought a DVD, took some pictures, and gathered some pamphlets and the spirits of Scarlett O'Hara, Jane Austen, and Laura Ingalls, before we headed out the door.

Chapter 16

BLACK PEPPER

On a walk with my son and our four-legged, Teddy, I saw a sign that an eighteen-month-old black cat named Pepper was lost. I remembered the collar I found yesterday when cleaning the garage in preparation for my in-laws coming over for a barbecue. I thought the very tiny collar belonged to a very tiny dog. I picked it up and placed it on the stove in the garage, made a note in my head to call the number on the collar, then forgot about it.

"I'll call them when I get home," I told my son.

At the park, we ran into my brother and his dog, Prince. We walked with them, and then hung out at my brother's house for a little while. I sat in the backyard that faced the park, separated only by a fence, while my son played with my great-nephew. Teddy needed to rest. It was a humid day in late May. My brother and I chatted a bit and then he left to pick up food from the brother's house who lives across the street from me. I meditated under a tree I know not the name of, for my parents didn't tell me all about trees, nor birds and bees, but no matter, I still took comfort there until my brother returned and my son said, "I want to go home."

At home, I called the cat's owner, Mira. She appeared as quickly as a genie, not that I've met a genie before or know how swift they can appear or disappear. She was blonde and petite with a beautiful face, probably in her late fifties, early sixties. She carried a stuffed pink-and-white monkey named

"Monkey" and a cat carrier. My daughter and niece said they had seen Pepper a few days ago at Naser's house, my next-door neighbor. Marla and I went to Naser's backyard, and we used her flashlight and my iPhone to look for the cat. The neighbor's house had a shed and a huge tree I know not the name of. I'm most familiar with date palm trees that flourish throughout and dominate the landscape of southern Iraq, though I've enjoyed picking apples from apple trees, mulberry from mulberry trees, pears from pear trees, peaches from peach trees, and so on and so forth.

"I saw a black cat pass by a few hours ago," said Ghaida, the neighbor behind my house and Teddy's second mother.

Marla and I walked toward her and the three of us met at the fence that separated us.

"Teddy barked at it," she continued.

Marla looked at Teddy and asked him, "Teddy, have you seen Pepper?"

Teddy said nothing.

Marla took my number, address, and fingerprints (just kidding), and she thanked me profusely for caring about her cat. She said if not for the condition we were in, the COVID-19 pandemic, she'd hug and kiss me. She was relieved now that she had hope of seeing Pepper again. Then she vented about her ex.

"My husband—well, we divorced six years ago," she said. "He's very negative and when we looked for the cat together yesterday, he kept telling me he knows they'll never find Pepper now that seventy-two hours have passed. He was verbally abusive and I told him to shut up. He's a very good man but was raised in a dysfunctional family."

A middle-aged man with a sheepish smile appeared from around the garage corner and remained there. Marla didn't bother to glance at his direction as she vented for quite some time. He patiently waited and I listened with glorious calm in order to help soothe her hurt and pain. The pandemic, along with my age, was making me think more about how I treat others. It reminded me to enjoy participating in the Golden Rule: Do unto others as you would have them do unto you. I went to bed, grateful for the community I lived in which believed in this Golden Rule.

While everyone slept, I lay on the bed with eyes wide open and thought how prior to the late 1700s, there is little written history about the area that is now Sterling Heights. The Indian tribes who lived in villages along the Clinton River, or came through here on hunting expeditions, did not keep written records. They were mainly the Wyandotte, Chippewa, and Ottawa Tribes and they had thrived in the region from around 9000 BC until 1860, when white inhabitants and disease had threatened and diminished the Native American population.

I imagined the time when, for thousands of years, the Indians roamed the area. They lived along the Clinton River, formed over 20,000 years ago from the expansion and recession of huge glaciers throughout the area. Once known as the Huron River, the original Indian name of the river was Natawasippee, the Clinton River received its current name back on July 17, 1824. It was renamed in honor of the New York governor, DeWitt Clinton. Area pioneers hunted the abundant game in the lush forests along the river and had no problems catching fish in its clear, fast running water.

I paused, halfway through my thoughts and imagination, as a sudden hunger to enter their era ached my gut. I closed my eyes and saw complete darkness before a tanned woman appeared. She had luminous eyes and thick long hair the color of raven wings. She sat cross legged on elk hides, barely clothed, a large bowl between her thighs, her hands scooping some type of dry grain. "Sit down, daughter," she said to me.

"Who are you?" I asked.

"Long ago, I lived on this land, and was given power to fight for our world, for our people as terrible times filled with blood and sorrow came," she said. She stared at me. "Sit down. You're still standing."

I sat on dirt floor before a fire that I hadn't noticed or felt until now.

"Listen while I talk," she said and told me how, once upon a time, there were plentiful resources along this river that included deer, bears, wild turkeys, rabbits, weasels, minks, grouse, and partridge. This was the chief reason for the area's early development.

My mind, oblivious of the physical world, floated between information this woman shared and that which I read in stacks of books. I once came across research where scholars at the University of Michigan claim that the first inhabitants of the land hunted, fished, and lived on these fertile grounds more than eleven thousand years ago. Artifacts found in the early 1960s at Holcombe Beach show that Paleo Indians were here as early as 9,000 BC. The archaeological site formed millions of years ago is near the intersection of Metropolitan Parkway and Dodge Park Road in Sterling Heights. It's where scientists eventually found more than seven thousand arrowheads and flint chips. The Paleo-Indians, or the classification given to the first Native Americans that inhabited the Americas, hunted so much and so frequently here that they played a large role in the extinction of mammoths and caribou in the Great Lakes Region. These Indians also played a key role in bringing the first white inhabitants of the region, many who were captives of the Chippewa Indians and were either freed or had escaped their captors.

Teddy barked, wanting to be let outside. I opened my eyes, and the tanned woman disappeared into thin air. I got out of bed and let Teddy out, then sat on the burgundy uphol-stered armchair in the living room while waiting for him to return so I could let him in. He took a long time as he some-times does when wanting to just chill on the porch, stare at the shining stars in the sky and keep an eye out for the animals that crossed our backyard at night, such as racoons and cats. My head pressed against the chair's inside wing, I traveled far away in a magnificent dreamland. All I saw was a delightful vi-sion of when apple, peach, and mushroom orchards dotted the landscape of this area, thousands of sheep and cows graced on rich grasslands, and hundreds of horses worked the fields. The meals commonly contained rhubarb in some form, as this was the main crop of farmers at the time. Most rhubarb was grown in sheds or small buildings known as "hothouses" instead of being grown outside. This established Macomb County as the "rhubarb capital of the world" in the mid-1800's.

Over the centuries, not much changed in the lifestyles of the inhabitants of the township; church and farming were prioritized for the close-knit families in the community. By the 1880s, the township had become thirty-six square miles of well-developed and prosperous farms, with a mere thou-sand residents. Boys and girls were so busy doing chores and roaming in the pastures that there was little time for chit-chat-ting. The only time children attended school was after all the crops were harvested, the livestock tended to, and the day's work was complete.

People walked to school. They walked to town. They shared and helped one another. With the help of neighbors and relatives, farmers in the township were able to harvest their crops very quickly and efficiently, with the host family usually serving a meal to those who helped. People had a gen-eral optimism toward the world around them, had a sense of community and a simple philosophy about life. The Golden Rule and the Bible were their guide to a decent life.

I remembered Father Bazzi's description of my ancestral village's harvest season. In his book *The Life of Tilkepnaye*, he writes that many farmers harvested barley, lentils or fava beans, and cucumbers. They traveled to-and-fro on foot, donkeys, horses, or wagons pulled by a donkey or mule. "With them, the birds of the sky sang because some of the grains that fell left much food for the birds… Many prayed the rosary while they walked, and they sang religious poems, stories, and ballads—especially the story of the Virgin Mary."

Teddy barked, startling me from one of my trips, which resembled Dorothy's in *The Wizard of Oz*, a lovely, lovely movie that I had only recently watched, thanks to the pandemic slowing life down. The story was full of innocence and meaning. The relationship Dorothy had with her dog Toto meant so much to me, now that I have Teddy. Her desire to return home after a long, exciting journey was most appropriate during the time I watched it, when the world had disconnected from the hustle and bustle and enjoyed being home with family. After watching the film on a cold winter night, I had allowed myself to sleep on the couch and, like Dorothy, take a long shamanic journey to the most beautiful places so I can return home feeling rejuvenated.

The missing signs with Pepper's pictures doubled in the area. You saw them on every pole and tree, but now they were covered in plastic, because we'd informed Pepper's mom, Marla not Mira, I learned later, that the rain was destroying the paper. We'd often find Marla parked in front of our house, waiting in her car for Pepper to show up. He never did. We'd see her drive through the neighborhood and help her go into the backyards of homes of those neighbors we knew. Everyone was looking for Pepper. Once we caught sight of a black cat who wasn't a usual passerby and were certain it was Pepper. We called Marla, excited, and updated her. She asked if the hair was very fluffy. Pepper had very fluffy hair. Yes, we thought it was fluffy enough, or was it?

One night Marla came knocking on our door when my husband and I were getting ready to walk across the street to my brother's house where we were invited for dinner. My husband answered the door.

"Is your wife available?" she asked.

"Pepper's mother wants you," my husband said as I brushed my hair in front of the mirror.

"What did she say? Did they find Pepper?"

"She said, 'Is your wife available?'" he said, grinning.

I came to the door and she began to talk. My husband, knowing this would take a while, said he'd meet me at my brother's house and sauntered to the other side of the street. Marla talked for half-an-hour. She hadn't slept for days, was exhausted and earlier, felt dizzy and faint. I felt so bad for her and comforted her as much as possible, praying her cat would find his way home. Turns out that she was the owner of the one big dog I often saw behind the elementary school, in the backyard with the huge tumor on the side of her stomach. The dog was seventeen years old, she told me, and that was why they couldn't perform surgery on her. She was too old.

Marla left a pillow that Pepper liked to sleep on and beside it "Monkey" on my front porch's rocking bench. She also put a bowl of cat food and one of water to help lure Pepper to our doorsteps. Once she left, I walked across the street to my brother's house for a nice and quiet gathering. The cat food led to a number of stray cats visiting our front yard, putting Teddy in a frenzy that woke me up several times during the night. They ate to their heart's content and moved on, roaming the streets once again.

The following night, my sister-in-law called while I was making dinner. She saw Pepper run across the street to our home. I rushed to the backyard and saw the neighbor getting ready to pick up Teddy from our side of the fence. My daughter and I caught sight of Pepper at the neighbor's and called his name. "Pepper! Pepper!"

He looked at me and ran. I called Marla and she appeared within thirty seconds, her friend, the ex, beside her. The ex stayed a good distance back, impishly looking in our direction. My husband and I talked with her for a while, and to ease her anxiety, told her that Pepper looked like he was having a good time. "I'm more concerned about you than him," I said.

We laughed a lot and I told them to go home, relax, and have a nice dinner together. Maybe they're meant to get back together? Pepper seems to be happy on the street and hanging out with the cats next door. She, on the other hand, needs her friend / ex-husband and he looks like he loves her. Her seventeen-year-old dog with a tumor will not last long. Marla needs a companion, a human one.

She laughed, said he's a good man, but once again raged about his inadequacies. After she left, I did yoga for forty-five minutes while watching with my husband the Saudi movie *Barakah Meets Barakah* and then *90 Day Fiancé*. The neighbors called. Teddy threw up so we went to pick him up from over the fence.

Days passed and we never stopped looking for Pepper. Whenever we saw a black cat, we assumed it was him, took a video and shared it with Marla. She said, "No, that's not him. Pepper is dark black."

Then one day I received a call from Marla telling me she'd found Pepper crying under a car. Someone had seen the missing sign and said this one cat was under the car for days. She rushed to him, and they reunited. Then she drove to our home to show us Pepper and pick up his toy "Monkey" as well as his pillow and food bowls. Teddy so desperately wanted to get his paw on Pepper, but of course, we didn't let him. He was just fuming, his nostrils flaring in excitement. The important thing was that Pepper was found, and when we shared the good news with everyone in a group chat, along with pictures of Marla elatedly holding Pepper, we typed "kululululu"—a traditional Middle Eastern mirth that women make during happy occasions and celebrations.

CHAPTER 17

CRANBROOK HOUSE AND GARDENS

In an attempt to busy my mind, change environments, and feel of use, I registered for a Cranbrook House and Gardens docent training orientation. The email invitation read, "We encourage those with strong communication skills and an interest in art, architecture, and history to join our docent program." That would be me, right? I majored in communication and had an interest in art, architecture, history, and of course, storytelling. It was a volunteer position, but it would keep my mind off the loss of my mom.

In the dark hour, I arrived at the concrete house that looked like an old English cottage. I walked into a foyer, where I removed my coat and boots, and walked through the glass double doors, then into the reception room that expands into numerous other rooms. A table in the corner, with a few lamps behind it and a China display cabinet next to it, had stacks of pamphlets about the house and its owners, George and Ellen Scripps Booth. The couple moved in with their five children from Detroit to their built home in 1908. Married for twenty-one years, they became the first year-round residents of means of that un-incorporated farming area which today is known as Bloomfield Hills, one of the wealthiest and most beautiful cities in Michigan.

I wrote my name on the registration form on the table. Then I was led with the other docents-in-training to what was referred to as the common room or music room. Over a dozen of us sat around long tables set up, it seemed, for meetings, classes, or other activities. I sat down and observed the low vaulted plaster ceiling, the linenfold paneling around the walls, and the numerous portraits. The woman leading the docent training introduced herself and shared stories about George and Ellen. In 1887, a man named George Booth married a woman named Ellen Scripps. George was an owner of a successful iron-working company in Windsor, Ontario, and Ellen was the eldest child of James Scripps, the founder of the *Detroit Evening News,* today known as *The Detroit News.* George was given an opportunity in 1888 to join the Scripps family's empire and took it. He then worked closely with his father-in-law to build the newspaper into Detroit's largest daily. He was also a founding member of the Detroit Institute of Arts.

It wasn't long before my imagination took off to Ellen's father, who built a house for the couple across from his own on Trumbull Avenue in Detroit. They enjoyed living there yet longed to have a large estate in the country. In 1904, they made their dreams come true by purchasing a run-down 174-acre farm in Bloomfield Hills and named it Cranbrook, after the English town the Booth family came from. They began cultivating the property by laying in roads, marking hillsides, creating lakes, establishing farm buildings, and starting a huge planting campaign to cover the barren rolling terrain. For the first few years, the Booths spent only their summers at Cranbrook. Winters were spent in their Detroit home where George began to develop plans for the family's country residence.

The family lived in this house for forty years where they raised their children and managed their farm. They created what would eventually become the Cranbrook Educational Community, an education, research, and public museum complex that consisted of six institutions. This includes Cranbrook Academy of Art, the nation's top-ranked school dedicated entirely to education in art, architecture, craft, and design. On its website, the academy is described as "a truly radical experiment that hinges on the belief that extraordinary things can happen when people are given time and space to explore their work in a supportive and inclusive community."

It all sounded like a most heavenly place for artists who are self-motivated. Cranbrook students get to develop their own curriculum, and they don't have to deal with a grading system, someone taking attendance, or making sure they're participating. They get to decide how to spend and manage their time while given plentiful academic resources. They are provided with the space, community, and means that I as an independent writer and filmmaker had to provide for myself within the walls of my sacred room in the house built on the grounds of "Little Baghdad."

But there was a sad ending to part of the story. The house in Detroit was later gifted by James Scripps to the city of Detroit and became the Scripps branch of the Detroit Public Library at Trumbull Avenue and Myrtle Street. The branch closed in 1959 and was demolished in 1966. Even its Gothic tower was later demolished despite the Booth's youngest son, Henry, attempting to save it. Today the area is Scripps Park. In trying to learn why this branch of the library was destroyed, I stumbled upon another story of no better ending; the Mark Twain branch of the Detroit Public Library was demolished in 2011 after decades of neglect.

I wanted to ask questions, such as, why were such important buildings demolished? But who would I ask? The landowner, the City of Detroit, the library, or perhaps a Booth family member? How would I even track down any of them? I doubt their names could be found in the yellow pages. And who uses those anymore?

"This dining table can expand to eighteen chairs when

needed," said the docent trainer, waking me up from my burning questions and into the Booth's fancy dining room. "If you notice, only George and Ellen's chairs had finials because one night at dinner the maid caught her sleeve in the corner of the chair and spilled soup into the lap of one of the Booth's sons. The next day a man was brought in to saw off all the rest of the finials so the maid's sleeve would never again get caught on the chair."

I wondered what type of soup they were having and whether when it spilt on the boy, it caused any real damage or just loads of unwarranted drama. Did the incident disrupt the meal, or did the family address the spilt soup matter-of-factly and then simply continue eating with delight? And by the way, what did their dinner consist of? Their lunch and breakfast? Was the food always gourmet and included spring greens and specialty desserts or were meals ever simple and made of hamburger and fries, followed by scoops of ice cream?

As I envisioned the meals that took place around the dining table, I heard the docent explain that we were each assigned a script with a room to memorize for the next meeting. Each week, we'd play docent as a means to attaining true docent status. Fear crept in. I don't retain information very well unless the topic truly matters to me. Otherwise, I tend to freeze. And lo and behold, that was exactly what happened when I stood there in the center of puzzled looks from the rest of the docents-in-training, unable to recall anything about the dining room except that the maid spilt soup on one of the sons and Mrs. Booth's silverware had "Nelly" etched on the reverse of each of the pieces, the name that her family called her. This reminded me of Nelly Olson in *Little House on the Prairie.*

That night, walking to my car in the cold quiet winter

night, I reflected on the house. The large private library where one of the Booth's daughters had her wedding reception intrigued me. They had parties and concerts there as well. There were windows that overlooked the gardens which were never visible to us, given the evening hours we had to meet. Mr. Booth's "Still Room" where he went to be still or take a nap, had candlesticks of Adam and Eve, and a ceiling made by a famous New York sculpture, Ulysses Ricci. The ceiling was shipped to Michigan by train and installed onto the wall. Then one of the Booth's sons hand-painted it Michelangelo style, by rigging up a seat on his back. The tapestry in the house was magnificent. One of them had General Pershing in the center leading the doughboys in from America, named doughboys because of the buttons on their uniforms looked like little puffs of dough.

By the time my feet reached my car, I'd made up my mind. I can't do this.

At home, I emailed the trainer, explaining that while I enjoyed the two training sessions at Cranbrook House and Gardens, I realized I'm not currently suitable for this task. My mother recently passed away and it seemed that I haven't yet wrapped my head around the changes that has brought. She graciously responded:

Hello Weam,

First, I'm so sorry to hear you have recently lost your mom. Mothers are very special, especially to daughters. I know you have special memories you will cherish forever. I totally understand if this is not the right time for you to go through the docent training class. Please know you are always welcome, and we look forward to your return.

Thank you,
Joyce

I tucked away the idea of being a docent and forever put it to rest. I'd have to find another little adventure to help get me out of my sorrow, or maybe the adventure would find me. And just like that, not even two months later, I received a call from Judy introducing herself as the chairperson of the Chaldean Cultural Center. She saw my name in the foreword I'd written for the book *101 Questions and Answers About Chaldean Americans, their Religion, Language and Culture*, published by Michigan State University one day before my mother's death on February 6, 2019. She'd never heard of me before, and reading my bio, was impressed I'd published thirteen books.

"Fourteen," I said. "My recent book was released in January."

Judy invited me to visit the Chaldean Museum. I agreed not so much for the museum, but because she was a certified energy healing practitioner who hosted and led group meditations. This was rare to see in the Chaldean community. I thought I was the only one who openly claimed such a title.

Between the docent training and Judy calling me, a lot had happened. I'd sold for a small cost my mother's hospital bed to someone who really needed it and donated the money to my mother's niece in Iraq. I returned her brand-new leased wheelchair, which I worked so hard to get her for Christmas, to the medical equipment store. I got a new puppy who turned my life around. I began to feel my mother's presence through butterflies that fluttered around me especially when I was feeling down. As promised, I'd brought Babba's casket next to my mother's grave on April 9 and four days later, Detroit Working Writers (DWW) had its annual meeting at Shield's Bar and Pizzeria. We were going to cast our vote for Election of Officers and Honorary Directors. My name was on the 2019 ballet for president, alongside the then current president Roberta Brown.

At the time, I was vice president of DWW, the oldest writing organization in Michigan which was established in 1900 by thirteen professional women journalists and literary writers. It changed names a few times and from 1966 until 2004, it was known as Detroit Women Writers. DWW board members had wanted me to run a second two-year term as vice president and asked if I'd consider declining the nomination for presidency. I said no, knowing that I was built to be a leader and grow in that role, not remain in one spot for too long or take steps backwards.

I lost the election by a landslide and was extremely relieved. For fifteen years, I had volunteered my time to a number of nonprofits and felt that I'd paid my dues with little or even no appreciation in return. My skills and talents, along with my education, experience, and the desire to inspire, motivate, and lead people deserved a position that deserved me. I wanted a place that gave and not just received, as any healthy relationship should be based on, whether it was husband and wife, child and parent, employer and employee.

So when Roberta called the next day, showing sympathy about how "disappointed I must be about the results," I responded, "No, I'm not disappointed at all! I'm very happy for you. I am a faith-based person, like you, so I believe that things happen for a reason. Obviously, I am not meant to be the president of Detroit Working Writers. You are!"

I meant what I said to Roberta, but afterward, I felt a disconnect from the group, so I bowed out by not renewing my yearly membership. I wanted to move on. Where to? I wasn't sure. But something else was calling me, and in order to hear what that something had to say, I had to stand still, to listen, to see, what I was to do next.

These were the events that happened between my

mother's passing and my meeting with Judy that gloomy cold day in May at the Chaldean Cultural Center.

After Judy gave me a tour of the museum, where I floated along spontaneous streams of consciousness and visited with my mother near the Ziggurat, I walked out of Shenandoah feeling better. The sand I'd walked upon had quenched my thirst. It felt as if I'd taken communion with fresh grape juice and sacramental bread. I felt better than when I walked in, but I did not feel full. I wanted to further taste the five galleries that transported me to my ancestral home and made me feel that I belong.

In the car, as I drove out of the parking lot, I called my husband. I told him I'd just seen the world's first and only Chaldean Museum, and that, contrary to what I'd heard from some naysayers, it's very beautiful. It moved me. I wanted to return to it one day and linger for hours on my own, to reflect and savor the moments. But no more than that.

"They're looking for an executive director," I said. "I think that's why I was invited."

"Forget about it," he said, and suggested I should never work with Arabs or Chaldeans. I agreed, knowing from experience what it meant to work for the Middle Eastern community. Once you said "yes," you committed as deeply as you did to responsibilities associated with your family members. A thirty-hour-per-week job, the requirement for a CCC executive director, really meant double that number. I recalled Roberta's list of to-dos for Detroit Working Writers. She constantly mentioned how she put more hours of work as a volunteer than at her paying job. Even though the CCC's position was paid, I did not want to deal with office politics, a dreadful workload, and arriving home exhausted with no energy or time left for a personal life.

"Plus, I can't leave Teddy all alone," I said, piling onto the list. "He's just a baby."

I arrived home, anxiously rushed out of the car, and walked through the door to a happy and excited four-pound Teddy. I could not get over the way in which he was thrilled each time he saw me or any of our family members. He wiggled his tail and did a little dance, jumping up and down, left and right, looking like a mixture of a bunny and a belly dancer. For him, loved ones seemed to be the most important thing in the world. He portrayed an uninhibited selfless love that even mothers could not sustain on such an around-the-clock consistent basis.

I scooped Teddy in my arms, hugged and played with him before I began preparing lunch for the kids so it was ready before picking them up from school. I had a busy schedule and no, by no means was I going to start working somewhere that required a forty-five-minute drive.

Weeks passed. Judy called one day wanting to do a community film screening at the Maple Theater for my documentary, *The Great American Family*, which had won two international awards. In return, I invited to interview her and Mary Romaya, the executive director of the CCC, on my cable TV show. The ladies arrived looking beautiful; Judy wore a green jacket over a white blouse and Mary had on a red jacket that accentuated her reddish hair. We settled into the small solo studio and before I began recording, Judy once again mentioned that they were looking for an executive director. I said it would be a good idea to mention that during the interview. Then I hit the record button and the show began.

As they talked, the experience I had when I first entered the museum reappeared. The spirits of my parents and grandparents danced in that small soundproof room, taking hold of my thoughts and feelings, reminding me of where I came from and why it mattered to process our past and shed light on it. As a storyteller, it was a vital lifetime commitment to learn about and appreciate what my ancestors were up against, how they handled things, got to the other side, and prospered. This was an opportunity for understanding why we have certain characteristics, healing old wounds, and transforming our narratives.

For decades, I and other Chaldean writers and artists have complained that our Chaldean community does not really have a hub that promotes art and culture. Even though the center was established in 2003, one of its main focuses was building the boutique museum. The 2008 recession caused funds to dry up and further delay was caused by the massive amount of effort put into it. Thousands of photos were collected and hundreds of people were interviewed. Each story and each fact was researched, checked, and double-checked to assure accuracy. As a result, it took fourteen years to finally open the museum in 2017.

The founders did an amazing job establishing what they called the CCC's "little gem." But then what? What about programing, outreach, and sustainability? All of which are challenging for any arts and culture endeavor, but especially for societies that have been led by dictatorships who wanted to erase the stories of indigenous and minority groups.

Dictatorships don't value the arts because they fear creativity and they want everyone to conform. That, along with capitalism, has caused our community to care a lot more about getting their hair and nails professionally done and outdoing each other with the house, the diamond ring, car model, or brand names of their clothes. Showing off is a priority, and so is tattooing your eyebrows and injecting your lips and other body parts, carrying certain brand-name purses and shoes to match. Putting on a façade of wealth and sophistication was an ongoing trend. The days of polishing your own nails and sticking your hand out the car window is for the remaining few, such as myself and some of my sisters. When I have a wedding of a close relative, like that of a niece, nephew, or first cousin, I'm always asked, "Who's going to do your hair? Who's going to do your makeup?" Naturally, I am.

The time most women take to get ready for a wedding, I could finish writing a book chapter! What I love to do is so beyond many of my loved ones' comprehension, that I get an earful of useless suggestions that I pretend to agree with just so I don't waste time getting more of an earful of useless suggestions. Then I go along and do what makes me happy, and what makes me happy is often locked up in my psyche until I share it through my writing, most of which is not read by those who think they know me. In more recent years, my busy schedule, along with my enormous accomplishments, has caused some of the earful useless suggestions to lessen.

During the interview I learned that Mary and Judy were born here, as was Judy's mother. Neither women knew Arabic or Aramaic, nor had they ever visited Iraq. In our conversation, I acknowledged the worthiness of their cause, and how as a writer, I too felt it important to inform the world about our heritage, language, and culture given the Islamic State efforts to destroy it before our very eyes. The spirits in the room kept dancing, tapping the buttons of my heart, and trapping me into stillness long enough to see the vision that had been in front of me all along. It felt something similar to when I met my husband, four years after our initial encounter, and knew that he and I would spend the rest of our lives together. He, on the other hand, recognized me as his soulmate from our first encounter.

The drive home that night was different than any other after an interview. I felt melancholy, having met the future I had thought had nothing to do with me. I'd traveled the world to get away from anything related to being Chaldean only to end up in the heart of everything that was. While marriage and children caused me to embrace my home and neighborhood, the truth was that I felt comfortable with the way my family does "Chaldean." I did not enjoy dealing with Chaldeans outside the borders of my home and community. The new situation triggered negative feelings I had toward my people's dark side, a side which I'd worked hard to insulate and isolate myself from. Yet here I was, considering a position I didn't think I would ever sign up for.

How could this be, and what did this mean? Having the talent or experience, or even the interest, didn't mean having the will to lead. I prayed on the question during a full moon ceremony, where friends and I sat around a bonfire, wrote our wants and desire as well as whatever we wanted to release from our lives, and threw the paper into the fire. Tears rushed down my face as the truth took hold of me. The superficial expectations washed from my body and mind, stilling me, as I saw the next phase in my life; being a leader in an area that needs that leadership. Surrender, I kept hearing, to what is about to come.

The next few weeks were exhausting yet also fulfilling and humbling all at once. It was clear what I had to do. Judy had invited me to lunch and offered that I pick the restaurant. I chose Bahama Breeze Island Grille. My husband and I went there often, sometimes alone, other times with our children and relatives. We enjoyed the outdoor seating area, the live Caribbean music during the weekends and the happy hour during the week.

"Would you like anything to drink?" the waitress asked.

"I'll have a Mojito Cubano," I said, remembering the last time I ordered this tasty drink which had rum, sugarcane, lime juice and fresh mint leaves. After we placed our food order and the waitress took our menus and left, it hit me that it was still daylight. "I don't drink during this hour," I said, confused. "But because I normally come here at night with my husband, I ordered it out of habit."

She laughed. "That's okay."

My drink arrived shortly afterward, followed by a plate of "Tequila Sunburn Glazed Salmon," topped with pineapple-mango salsa, and served with cinnamon mashed sweet potatoes and green beans. I savored the food as Judy and I shared how we got involved in energy healing work, the traumas that we experienced in life, how we juggle things as wives and mothers, and how we remain focused. I was reluctant to tell her the answer she'd been stalking, that I accept the job as CCC's executive director. Leadership required a lot of responsibility, 150 percent commitment, and once committed, it was unlikely that I could get out of it. I took commitments quite seriously. It was a demanding job that required patience, strength, the ability to treat people fairly, and to make tough decisions for the benefit of the greater good, even if others consider it otherwise…

"Is everything okay here? Can I get you anything else?" the smiling waitress asked.

"No, we're good," Judy and I responded.

The clock was ticking. My eyes watched the sun rays that shed light over our table and the dust particles within them. It gave me a warm and cozy feeling.

"I've been thinking about the executive director position…" I began, slowly.

Judy's eyes widened, knowingly and with excitement. Not much more needed to be said. The deal was sealed. A sense of delight entered our mood and atmosphere. Judy expressed her happiness about the news and soon afterward got up and grabbed the check. "I'll get that," she said. "I have another meeting, but we'll talk."

She left in a hurry and I remained seated, finishing my drink and watching the sun rays and the dust particles. "Brati, you did the right thing," the voice of my mother pierced through my heart, blessing me in her native tongue and wrapping me like a blanket as I stared ahead and prepared my emotions for the change.

My first day at the job was October 1, 2019, and eight days later was my film screening. Tickets sold out. Immediately afterward, I began to use my communication skills, decades of experience in nonprofits, and my interest in art, history, and storytelling to document my ancestors' heritage, culture, and language. Maybe to even preserve it, while acknowledging diversity and celebrating various heritages. Throughout my career, I didn't feel supported as a writer because of my familial culture, Chaldean culture, and my American culture, which although has a value for the arts, it doesn't understand the diverse backgrounds and experiences of Middle Easterners.

The drive to and from work every day was a special path. As seasons changed, I passed White Chapel Cemetery when, during the fall, I saw vividly colored leaves sprinkled over the ground, a few flying in the air; in the winter, the area was coated with glistening white snow and Christmas wreaths; in the spring, the dirt began to show, later to be decorated by Mother's Day paraphernalia; in the summer, the grass blossomed and Father's Day celebrations were around the corner. Sometimes on the way home, I drove into the cemetery, stepped out, and sat beside the graves of my parents just to have a chat. This always gave me heart.

On a few occasions, I took a different path and passed the Cranbrook House & Gardens, remembering the time when I wanted to partake in sharing my love for history. It didn't work out then, but it sort of led to where I belonged to do just that. As a docent at the Chaldean Museum, it didn't take long for me to passionately tell the history of the Chaldeans while living enjoyably and harmoniously among Jews, Muslims, and Christians, the way it was for hundreds of years in the remote Kurdish region of northern Iraq until the late 1940s. I even put on a performance where at the end I've received numerous ovations in the form of applause. Inspired by many, including George Booth, I embraced my unique position, and in return, offered a unique perspective. After all, I have a role that no other person in the world has because there is no other Chaldean Museum. It is in this space that I can stroll into the past, into the unthinkable knowledge and force of the Mesopotamians, and remain still in their timeless silence. Then in a state of magical and mystical control, I drive seventeen miles home to "Little Baghdad," with the freedom to direct my own story.

NOTES

Introduction

Living Tribal in a Democracy
www.livingtribalinademocracy.com

Chapter 1

Weam Namou, "It's Never Too Late: New American is 111 years old," *The Chaldean News* (February 1, 2012), pg. 34

Clifton B. Parker, "Research: The Hidden Benefits of Gossip and Ostracism," (February 5, 2014) www.gsb.stanford.edu/ insights/research-hidden-benefits-gossip-ostracism

Claire Jeantet and Fabrice Catérini, *My Beloved Enemy: Iraqi American Stories*
my-beloved-enemy.inediz.com/?a=391 [Detroit] Shamamta

Weam Namou, "Spotlight on Refugees: 'My Beloved Enemy' makes its American debut this month," The Chaldean News (December 1, 2013), pg. 36

Edward Cody, "Iraqis Must Learn to Read and Write—Or Else!" *Washington Post* (September 27, 1979)

Chapter 3

Weam Namou, "Seven Mile Blues: 'Chaldean Town' Continues to Struggle," *The Chaldean News* (May 1, 2009), pg. 26-27

Jovan Kassab, "Life Along Seven Mile: The first U.S. home for many faces its challenges," *The Chaldean News* (October 1, 2006), pg. 34-35

Rachel Aviv, "Saddam Hussein's Key to the City of Detroit" www.bidoun.org/articles/saddam-hussein-s-key-to-the-city-of-detroit

"Table 6—Crimes in the United States 2007" www2.fbi.gov www2.fbi.gov/ucr/cius2007/data/table_06.html

"Table 6—Crime in the United States 2008" www2.fbi.gov www2.fbi.gov/ucr/cius2008/data/table_06.html

Tom Perkins, "Review: Sullaf Iraqi restaurant is the last man standing in Detroit's 'Chaldean Town'—and it's awesome" (May 2, 2018) www.metrotimes.com/food-drink/chaldean-towns-last-man-standing-sullaf-iraqi-restaurant-is-chaotic-and-delicious-11683868

Chapter 4

C. Thomas, *Report on the Mound Explorations of the Bureau of Ethnology* (1894, report. 1985)

Chapter 5

Dr. Muqtedar Khan, "Prophet Muhammad's Promise to Christians," (August 22, 2010) www.ijtihad.org/prophet%20muhammed%27s%20promise.htm

Manuscripts in St. Catherine's Monastery, Mount Sinai www.loc.gov/collections/manu-scripts-in-st-catherines-monastery-mount-sinai/about-this-collection

John Andrew Morrow, *Islām and the People of the Book Volumes 1-3: Critical Studies of the Covenants of the Prophet—Volume 1*, (Cambridge Scholars Publishing, 2017), pg. 15

Weam Namou, "Wake up America: Detroiters Rally for Iraq's Christians," *The Chaldean News* (December 1, 2010) pg. 26-27

Weam Namou, "Voices of the Voiceless: Massacre remembrance takes added urgency," *The Chaldean News* (September 1, 2014), pg. 31

Dustin Block, "Video shows crowd cheering after mosque rejected in Sterling Heights," www.mlive.com/news/detroit/2015/09/video_shows_crowd_cheering_aft.html (September 11, 2015)

Tresa Baldas, "Feds Sue Sterling Heights for rejecting mosque; call move anti-Muslim," *Detroit Free Press* (December 15, 2016)

Niraj Warikoo, "Proposed mosque in Sterling Heights stirs opposition," *Detroit Free Press* (September 9, 2015)

Weam Namou, "Detained to be Deported: Members of the Chaldean community rounded up by ICE," *The Chaldean News* (July 1, 2017)

Weam Namou, "Fighting to Stay: Leaders in the community work to stop the deportation," *The Chaldean News* (July 1, 2017)

Weam Namou, "Why Jimmy Al-Daoud's deportation and death hurts all Americans," *Religion News* (September 1, 2019) religionnews.com/2019/09/01/why-jimmy-al-daouds-deportation-and-death-hurts-all-americans

"A Brief History of Tea… in India" www.cafesrichard.com

Chapter 6

Steve Connor, "The Anatomy of a Whale," *BBC Earth*, www.bbcearth.com/news/the-anatomy-of-a-whale

Nour Rahal, "Local Iraqi-American film, novel aims to bring unity between Chaldean, Muslim communities," *Detroit Free Press* (March 22, 2021)

Leaman, Oliver, *Companion Encyclopedia of Middle Eastern and North African Film.* (London and New York, Routledge, 20003)

"How reopening of cinemas in Saudi Arabia has proved film-industry game-changer" www.arabnews.com/node/2041361/saudi-arabia

"Yemen: Digital Media" medialandscapes.org/country/yemen/media/digital-media

Bruce Haring, "Netflix Series 'Jinn' Sparks Uproar in Jordan Over Alleged 'Immoral Scenes'" (June 15, 2019) www.deadline.com

Michael Levitt, "How a new Netflix film exposed a simmering tension in Egyptian society" (February 3, 2022)

www.npr.org/2022/02/03/1077379012/
netflix-egypt-perfect-strangers-mona-zaki

Entertainment Media Uses in the Middle East: A six-Nation
Survey, Northwestern University in Qatar and Doha Film
Institute (April 16, 2014) www.mideastmedia.org

Chapter 7

Sarah Troop, "The Hungry Mourner," *Modern Loss* (July 2,
2014) modernloss.com/food-death/

"Iraqis Bury Their Dead in Cemetery Destroyed by ISIS"
www.ndtv.com/world-news/iraqis-bury-their-dead-in-ceme-
tery-destroyed-by-isis-1586289 (October 26, 2016)

Dr. Adhid Miri, "Back to Iraq Part II" *The Chaldean News* (June
1, 2022)
www.chaldeannews.com/features-1/2022/6/1/
back-to-iraq-part-ii

Chapter 9

Con Coughlin, "Saddam," *The New York Times* (December 15,
2002)

"Why Don't Jehovah's Witnesses Celebrate Birthdays?" www.
jw.org/en/jehovahs-witnesses/faq/birthdays/

"'Muslims imitating Christians will be punished on judgment
day': Deoband Maulana Abdul Qasmi calls birthday celebrations

'Haram'" (November 25, 2022) www.opindia.com/2022/11/birthday-celebration-is-haram-says-maulana-qasmi-of-deoband

Abu Dawud and Ibn Hibban, "Book 16, Hadith 35; The Comprehensive Book" www.sunnah.com

Jabir B. Abdullah, "Book 7, Hadith 55, Chapter 13, Keeping the Prayer and Khutbah Short www.sunnah.com

Quran, Surah Balad, No. 90 verse 10

Katherine Ripley, *9 Facts About the Shih Tzu*, Sept. 21, 2021 www.akc.org/expert-advice/dog-breeds/shih-tzu-facts/

Ṣaḥīḥ al-Bukhārī 3225, Ṣaḥīḥ Muslim 2106

Muhammad and the Dogs www.answering-islam.org/Silas/dogs.htm

Ali Hamedani, "The country where having a pet could soon land you in jail" BBC World Service (July 19, 2022) www.bbc.com/news/world-middle-east-62205744

Brian Pellot, "Puppy petting event prompts death threats in Malaysia," www.ReligionNews.com (October 23, 2014)

Jon Levine, "Palestinian mayor offers bounty to residents who kill stray dogs," *The New York Post* (November 5, 2022) nypost.com/2022/11/05/palestinian-mayor-offers-bounty-to-residents-who-kill-stray-dogs

Weam Namou, *Mesopotamian Goddesses: Unveiling your Feminine Power*, Chapter 10, (Michigan, Hermiz Publishing, Inc. 2019)

Chapter 10

Dr. Adhid Miri, "The Traditional Chaldean Weddings," *The Chaldean News* (February 1, 2021)

Helen Wilbers, "Middle-schoolers make Mesopotamia museum," (November 1, 2019) www.fultonsun.com/news/2019/nov/01/middle-schoolers-make-mesopotamia-museum/

Giovanni Garcia-Fenech From Babylon to Berlin: The rebirth of the Ishtar Gate, (March 27, 2014) www.artstor.org/2014/03/27/the-rebirth-of-the-ishtar-gate/

Chapter 11

Elizabeth Goring (2004). *Treasures from Tuscany: the Etruscan legacy, Edinburgh*: National Museums Scotland Enterprises Limited. Pg. 13.

"Soap's history: 94bhandmade.pl/en/content/17-very-short-with-a-long-history-of-soap

Flood in Tel Keppe religion.fandom.com/wiki/Tel_Keppe

"No Longer Unknowable: Falluja's April Civilian Toll is 600" *Iraq Body Count* (October 26, 2004)

Chapter 12

"Woolley's Excavations" www.ur-online.org/about/woolleys-excavations

Emilienne Malfatto, "The Marsh Arabs of Mesopotamia" (January 18, 2017) roadsandkingdoms.com/author/emalfatto/ "Ziggurat of Ur" iraqheritage.org/cms.php?idp=45

Chapter 13

Daniel Strohl, "Fact Check: What Henry Ford meant when he said History is bunk'" www.hemmings.com/stories/2018/01/14/fact-check-what-henry-ford-meant-when-he-said-history-is-bunk

"The Meaning of 33: What it is and How to Use it" thewordcounter.com/meaning-of-33/

Geoffrey C. Upward, *A Home for our Heritage: The Building and growth of Greenfield Village and Henry Ford Museum, 1929-1979* (Henry Ford Museum Press, January 1, 1979) pg. 83

Adhid Miri, PhD, "Our Cousins, the Mandaeans: A look at the followers of John the Baptist," *The Chaldean News* *(October 1, 2022)*

"Israelite Communities Thruout the world," (June 27, 2015) losttentribes-tenlosttribes.blogspot.com/2015/07/israel-ite-communities-thruout-world.html

Fredrick Aprim, "The Mandaeans: True Descendants of Ancient Babylonians and Chaldeans," (April 24, 2013) www.mandaeanunion.com/history-english/item/489-descendents-of-ancient-babylonians-and-chaldeans

Erin Skarda, "Survey: People Aren't Happiest Until They Reach Age 33," *Time Magazine* (March 29, 2012)

Sandy Naimou, "Second-Generation Experiences of Ethnicity: Chaldean American Women in Metro-Detroit," (Thesis, Eastern Michigan University, October 2011) pg. 33

Chapter 14

Holger Gzella, "Aramaic, the English of the Levant in Antiquity," January 2015
bibleinterp.arizona.edu/articles/2015/01/gze398010

Iraqi Christians' long history (November 1, 2010)
www.bbc.com/news/world-middle-east-11669994

Ariel Sabar, "How to Save a Dying Language," (February 2013)
www.smithsonianmag.com/innovation/
how-to-save-a-dying-language-4143017

Roy Gessford, *Preserving the Chaldean Aramaic Language* (California, Let in the Light Publishing, 2020), pg. vii

Father Michael Bazzi, *The Life of Tilkepnaye: A 12 Month Study of Native Chaldean Catholics in Their Hometown of Tilkepe* (California, Let in the Light Publishing, 2021) pg. 30-31

Rose Eveleth "How to Revive a Lost Language" (February 8, 2013
www.smithsonianmag.com/smart-news/
how-to-revive-a-lost-language-13863932

Raymond Ibrahim, "Islamic Jizya: Fact and Fiction," (May 28, 2015) *FrontPage Magazine*

Chapter 15

Booklet on the Upton House Museum

"Telling The Sterling Story" SHTV1
www.youtube.com/watch?v=XCl_9bYSmL8

"Township History" www.sterling-heights.net/655/Township-History

Ruth Baker, *History of Sterling Heights*, Sterling Heights Public Library (March 1978)

Irene Courtney, *City of Sterling Heights* (December 27, 1973)

Sterling Township, 1875-1968, Arcadia Publishing (November 5, 2005)

Chapter 16
Cheri Gay, "Booth House + Scripps Land = Library" (July 23, 2013)
cranbrookkitchensink.com/2013/07/23/booth-house-scripps-land-library